The
South
Atlantic
Quarterly
Spring 1997
Volume 96
Number 2

The *South Atlantic Quarterly* (ISSN 0038-2876) is published
quarterly, at $75.00 for libraries and institutions and $28.00
for individuals, by Duke University Press, 905 W. Main
St., 18-B, Durham, NC 27701. Periodicals postage paid
at Durham, NC. POSTMASTER: Send address changes
to *South Atlantic Quarterly*, Box 90660, Duke University,
Durham, NC 27708-0660.

*Library exchanges* and orders for them should be sent to
Duke University Library, Gift and Exchange Department,
Durham, NC 27708.

The *South Atlantic Quarterly* is indexed in *Abstracts of En-
glish Studies, Academic Abstracts, Academic Index, America:
History and Life, American Bibliography of Slavic & East Euro-
pean Studies, American Humanities Index, Arts & Humanities
Citation Index, Book Review Index, CERDIC, Children's Book
Review Index (1965– ), Current Contents, Historical Abstracts,
Humanities Index, Index to Book Reviews in the Humanities,
LCR, Middle East: Abstract & Index, MLA Bibliography, PAIS,*
and *Social Science Source.* This journal is a member of the
Council of Editors of Learned Journals.

ISSN 0038-2876

ISBN for this issue: 0-8223-6444-1

# The Poetics of Derek Walcott:
# Intertextual Perspectives

SPECIAL ISSUE EDITOR: GREGSON DAVIS

The
South
Atlantic
Quarterly
Spring 1997
Volume 96
Number 2

**Gregson Davis**

The Poetics of Derek Walcott:
Intertextual Perspectives

The seven essays gathered in this special issue of *SAQ* offer discrete interpretations of the lyric oeuvre of anglophone Caribbean poet and Nobel laureate Derek Walcott. Three of these essays (Carol Dougherty's, Joseph Farrell's, and my own) focus critical attention on his monumental *Omeros*, while the remaining four (by Edward Baugh, Peter Burian, Judith Harris, and Timothy Hofmeister) explore important shorter poems from earlier collections in which some of the central, recurrent motifs of the longer poem are foreshadowed. Several of the contributors bring their specialized knowledge of the Greco-Roman literary tradition, especially of the Homeric epic, to bear on their nuanced discussions of individual poems. As is de rigueur with a poet as richly allusive as Walcott, intertextual perspectives predominate in this ensemble, with all the larger implications they entail for the situation of the postcolonial poet: the problematics of cultural identity in the Caribbean context, the assimilation of the Western canon, and the fluidity of the concept of literary genre, among others.

The scholarly essays are preceded by an edited transcript of a talk Walcott gave on *Omeros*

The *South Atlantic Quarterly* 96:2, Spring 1997.
Copyright © 1997 by Duke University Press.

during a visit to Duke University in the spring of 1995. The intimate tenor of the talk, which was informal and extemporaneous, was greatly enhanced by the presence in the room of an exhibit of paintings by the eminent African American artist Romare Bearden. Taking Bearden's images (in particular, his collages based on the *Odyssey*) as his point of departure, Walcott embarked on a wide-ranging conversation that shed light, inter alia, on his views concerning the centrality of narrative in art (pictorial as well as verbal) and the encomiastic dimension of *Omeros*. In the course of his talk and ensuing dialogue with the audience, he interspersed his reflections on his own work with insightful references to the craft of such canonic writers as Joyce, Shakespeare, and Dante.

In preparing the transcript of this memorable conversation for a larger audience of readers, I have attempted to preserve something of the intimate tone and colloquial style of the original, while making the editorial adjustments necessary to transform it from ad-lib oral performance to written text.

**Derek Walcott**

Reflections on *Omeros*

The strangeness of things this afternoon—and things get stranger as you get older, I think—is to be in this room to talk about *Omeros* and to have Romare Bearden's paintings here. I haven't yet had a chance to look at the exhibit, so these images provide me with great scope for a spontaneous association of ideas.

I shall begin with a kind of evocation of Romare's art, and of what it means for my own work. I don't think there's much difference between his work and that of a lot of artists who are rooted in a particular historical and cultural experience—not just the African American experience but the whole immigrant experience, or, for that matter, the whole American experience because that's what the immigrant experience essentially is. One of the most spectacular pieces of illustration, in my opinion, is Romare's set of collages based on the *Odyssey*. I'm not sure that it didn't influence me when I undertook to do that long poem [*Omeros*], which I had no idea was going to be so long, but which became longer because it was such a joy to work on. (It didn't get longer from necessity; it got longer from sheer elation. It was so very exciting to wake up in the

The *South Atlantic Quarterly* 96:2, Spring 1997.

morning just to get to work on it. It was also exciting for other reasons I hope I can describe to you today.)

I once used a cutout by Romare for the dust jacket of a volume of poems I called *The Star-Apple Kingdom* (1979). Look at that picture over there of a figure going down, like a diver in the sea. But Romare's genius had as much to do with his verbal ability to tell a story as his "scissors" ability to tell a story. I remember him describing an experience of being caught on a small boat between some islands in the Caribbean. He told of how the boat went adrift, and then he described the cargo, the pigs, the sailors, the people on board. And actually, even as I relate this anecdote about Romare, its referentiality immediately becomes Odyssean or Homeric because I just said "the boat, the pigs, the sailors," without any intention of sounding "Homeric" by alluding to the Circe episode and all that. These associations that occur naturally if you have read the Homeric poems (and not even read them well or thoroughly, but are merely evoking events in the context of the Caribbean) seem to me to register exact parallels, proportionally speaking, between the Caribbean experience and that of Homer's Greece—the scale of the thing. We think of the Trojan War as an epic directed by Spielberg, with two million extras; but when you think of what the actual scale of the walls of Troy was, or what size a Greek ship was, or the size of islands like Odysseus's "rock," Ithaca (which I have never visited, but that's the way he describes it), it turns out to be quite small. It's not on the scale of twentieth-century epic, which has more to do with size than spiritual width. To me, the *Odyssey* is not an epic in that sense; the *Odyssey* is a very domestic poem. It is a very small poem in idea. It's simply, obviously, the story of a man having a hard time getting home—a lot of it his own fault. I mean, if he came home twenty years after the end of the war and someone asked him, "What were you doing hanging out with Circe?" and he replied, "Oh well, you know how it is with goddesses," it would not be acceptable in that narrative context. {*laughter*} It's not a good enough story. And I don't want to take a feminist viewpoint, or any other kind of viewpoint, but just to say that this is rarely the hero's response. There's much more to it than "Hey, where have you been?"—"I went out for a pack of cigarettes and got caught up in the Trojan War, you know?" {*laughter*}

Every little thing you can think of as occurring today seems to have an ancient parallel. Of course, I don't think—and I'm sure I did not think— continually of parallels when planning *Omeros*. I did not plan this book so it would be a template of the Homeric original because that would be an absurdity. If you consider, for instance, the massive parallel that Joyce's *Ulysses* constitutes—the exact overlay, moment by moment, between *Ulysses* and the *Odyssey*, in which everything in Homer is echoed by the Irish experience—that's on a scale that no artist of today with any sensibility would attempt because then you would be doing a third version of the *Odyssey* via Joyce. You would have to start putting Black guys in, in place of White guys, and, you know, goats instead of pigs, and so forth. *Ulysses* remains a major twentieth-century *poem* because Joyce was a poet, he wrote like a poet. It's rather amazing that the major novel of our time *and*, perhaps, a major poem of our time should be *Ulysses*. You can take lines out of *Ulysses* that scan as poetry. A page of Joyce would be enough to make many a poet's career.

But to return to Romare's storytelling talent: when he was talking, he was a manifestly beautiful person, a genuinely beautiful person. This is how I met him: I was staying at the Chelsea Hotel [in New York], where a guy called Charles was in charge of things downstairs; he would go and get things for you. And one day he said, "There's somebody upstairs who wants to see you."

"Who is it?"

"Oh, you go ahead. You'll see who it is."

So I go upstairs, and there are two guys there. One is a sort of Buddha-like guy, with a bald head, and then there was another Black guy there. And I said to myself, "That's Romare Bearden. What's he doing in my room?" {*laughter*} So I sit down, and Romare sits down, and then his friend, the other painter, gently sits down as well. And we are looking at each other. So I think Romare must be thinking, "Well, didn't he invite us up here?" And I'm thinking, "I don't know how these guys got in here." Eventually, I said, "Well, what happened?" And Romare said, "I think Charles thought we should meet." So Charles the doorman arranged this historic meeting—"historic" in a funny sense.

As for Romare's story of traveling between islands on a boat, I wish, really wish, I had taken it down because it was beautifully told, just in terms of syntax. Now here's this man who lived in the Caribbean, on the island of St. Martin, who painted St. Martin and its people—an artist who owed a lot to Matisse, obviously, but who invented something that he has never really been credited for because he is Black, because this country is so limited in giving proper acknowledgment to its great Black artists. And I'm not making a polemic out of it; it's a fact. Romare's genius with the scissors was equivalent to Picasso's, in terms of his narrating and doing something that had the vibrations of his own experience, staying within the range of his experience. Well, there's no need to sound like that, but when you live in this country, they make you sound like that; you have to continually draw comparisons like "Lou Gossett is as good an actor as somebody else." That's the process and horror of living in this country, continually saying that the Black thing is as good as the White thing. But that, to me, was not the point about Romare. His genius consisted, first of all, in the astonishing skill he brought to cutting these figures out, and the astonishing sense of color—getting it right. To get that plasticity and volubility of the figure in the very process of cutting it out was astonishing.

Now what Romare did was not, for me, the kind of thing that many reviewers and critics saw in *Omeros*: a reinvention of the *Odyssey*, but this time in the Caribbean. I mean, what would be the point of doing that? What this implies is that geologically, geographically, the Caribbean is secondary to the Aegean. What this does immediately is to humiliate the landscape and say to the Caribbean Sea, "You must think of yourself as a second-rate Aegean, or, on a good day, you can look like the Mediterranean." {*laughter*} The stupid historicism of thinking that way leads some people to say that I also, as the author of *Omeros*, am trying to make it via Homer. I knew the book would provoke that kind of reaction; I also knew (and know) that nobody takes the last part of the book seriously. It's like saying to somebody, "When you worked at the bank, they said you took a lot of money. Is that true?"

"No, I didn't steal any money!"

"Okay."

Then the headline in the next day's paper reads "Man Accused of Stealing Money." Two months later—on page 10 of the paper—there is a two-line item: "Banker Exonerated." {*laughter*} If you look (if you take the trouble to look) at *Omeros*, you will see that the last third of it is a total refutation of the efforts made by two characters. First, there is the effort by the historian, Plunkett, to make a woman he has fallen in love with grander and nobler: the maid, Helen, who has worked for him—a beautiful Black woman, with terrific sensuality, that he has flipped over, and as a historian, he wants to give her a certain dignity, et cetera. But who is Plunkett to elevate this woman to a position of historical importance that is of no consequence to her, since history is of no consequence to her? And who is Plunkett to pronounce this benediction of elevation to a height that would make her the equal of a White Helen? A mistake. The second effort is made by the writer, or narrator (presumably me, if you like), who composes a long poem in which he compares this island woman to Helen of Troy. The answer to both the historian and the poet/narrator—the answer in terms of history, the answer in terms of literature—is that the woman doesn't need it. The conceit behind history, the conceit behind art, is its presumption to be able to elevate the ordinary, the common, and therefore the phenomenon. That's the sequence: the ordinary and therefore the phenomenon, not the phenomenon and therefore its cause. But that's what life is really like—and I think the best poets say that. It's there in Wordsworth; it's there in everyone: it is the ordinariness, not the astonishment, that is the miracle, that is worth recalling. It is not the war over Helen of Troy; it is Helen of Troy. It is not the invention; it is the person. It is not the country that's important; it is something that may embody the country. I think this is what really survives in great poetry. Now, this is not to say, "Oh, you did it differently; you won't be a great poet." But nobody looks at the point where my book pivots on itself and accuses itself of vanity, of the vanity of poetry, of the vanity of the narrator. There's a pivotal section that says: Why make an epic of two fishermen quarreling in a rum shop? Why do you have to make this so grand that you turn it into Hector and Achilles talking about Helen of Troy? Why do you need that? Why can't they just be two fishermen quarreling in a rum shop? Why do you have to make it sublime? Why do you have to make it heroic? Why do you have to make an epic out of it? Well, if you took that stance to the point where it actually worked, then there would be no need in life for metaphor. Then we would really *see*. And I think we would really see without that filter of the ego, without looking at things through the ego, through the palette of the ego, or through history, say, in the case of the writer who is contriving to tell this woman: "Look, you know, don't be bothered about being Black" (which is presumptuous and an oblique insult); "you mustn't worry about being Black, you know—you really are *as good as*." Now, however well-meant that is, in saying—as is often said to the Black person in this country—"You mustn't worry about being Black," there is a presumption that the Black person should be worried about it, but should ignore it. Therefore, the writer who says, "She is beautiful *but* Black, *but* she lives in the village," is doing the same thing. So these two forces—these two characters in *Omeros* are equally guilty of not arriving at that sublime mode that sees without edges and without references, which is what true poets have written about. You read in Rilke or in Pasternak, for example, or even in Larkin, of the wish to write a noun that has no echoes. Rilke says in the *Duino Elegies*, toward the end, as I recall, that he would like to be able to say—whatever—"water": How can I say it without all those things between me and that noun? Because between me and that noun there is already a history of the noun and therefore associations and references of that noun that I cannot get to. And this is true. It's there not only in Rilke, in Pasternak, and in Larkin, as I have said, but also in St. Paul, in the Epistle to the Corinthians; it's also in the clarity of the thing being itself, without being clouded or even having a shadow. When you get to Dante, to the *Paradiso*, the poet is saying that this is a world without shadows, a timeless world—because shadows regulate time. Shadows lengthen and shorten, and they can be registered on a dial that is representing time. In the last few cantos of the *Paradiso*, however, you come to a place in which there is light: light without heat, light without shadows, a steady radiance that consumes. But this consumption is not the devouring heat of, say, the sun but of a light that is, as Dante writes about it, *beyond art*. To get beyond art is the ideal of the artist, for anonymity is there.

Now, to speak in this way about the art of Romare Bearden seems very pompous as well as unduly prolonged, but I think people who look at Romare's collages of the *Odyssey* have to conclude that a Black artist is saying, "Okay, we can make this Black in this sense, that perhaps *x*, perhaps *y*." Romare's collages are to be seen as Egyptian, basically, not as if they are African American images. In other words, we are talking about a culture older than that of ancient Greece, a culture to which Greece owes a great deal of its mythology, among other things. And, therefore, it's not positing a Black Jesus or a Black Odysseus. The art in those collages represents what is antecedent to, or what precedes, our judgment of it as African or an adaptation, or whatever. How to see that is what's difficult because we would then have to go back to a kind of primal condition—unclouded by history, unclouded by academic association, unclouded by criticism. We would then have to see as simply as Romare's story does, to see a Greek port in which there would have been, let us presume, somebody called Homer, who was not just a guy drifting around playing a guitar or a lyre for money. Whether or not there was such a person, I myself have felt that you get a certain distance in the *Odyssey*, and you say to yourself, something is wrong here. In the second part of the *Odyssey*, the "prose" takes over, and this is not even recited; it is continuous, it doesn't end on a bar. And the rhythm of thudding on a beat—if you're thudding on a beat, don't go to a conjunction because that's not a stress. Perhaps you could say, oh well, that's just the translation, but I feel a distinct difference in style between, say, the naturalistic descriptions of the sea or the rocks or whatever in the first part and those in the second part of the *Odyssey*.

In terms of *Omeros*, I felt totally natural, without making it an academic exercise or a justification or an elevation of St. Lucians into Greeks, or some such nonsense, because of the harbors of the Caribbean, the work of the people in the Caribbean, the light in the Caribbean. I don't know the Greek islands, but that sense of elation you get in the morning, of a possibility that is always there, and of the width of the ocean—that, to me, is Caribbean first of all. Then too there are very few emblems—in literature and, I think, in all art. There are perhaps one or two iconic emblems that remain. One of them is, of course, somebody shouting at God, somebody uttering some virtual expletive at God. This is the source of all rebellious figures, so that in essence the defiance of God, of saying to God, "Screw you, I don't take orders from anybody, I am *X* or *Y*," begins with Lucifer, continues through Prometheus, through Daedalus, through Faust, through any number of figures who reject God's authority. And this is an emblematic, iconic figure. Very few icons have been created by the writer without legend.

Now here's what I mean: *The Odyssey* is the story of some man who wandered around, and the story of wandering is the classical epic. Epic is about wandering in search of something and finding (or not finding) it. You know, the knight leaves, goes forth and encounters different dragons, et cetera, on his quest. Then there's his return, or failure to return, just like with Odysseus. What we have because of Homer, *permanently* because of Homer (and without even having to read the book, already knowing that there is such a figure), are two emblems, at least. One is the Most Beautiful Woman in the World: Helen. That's indestructible, iconic, permanent for all cultures that share this part of history. The other emblem, of course, is the moving sail, alone on the ocean, not a ship but something small on a large expanse of water, trying to get somewhere—the image of the wanderer (call him Odysseus) made emblematic by the great poet. So what we have, then, at the core of the *Odyssey* is a figure traveling in a certain direction, trying to get home, through storms, et cetera. A lot of people tend to think of the *Odyssey* as a poem with a lot of monsters and a lot of things happening. But there aren't that many incidents, really, and they take up relatively little of the narrative content. And these stories obviously come from a very superstitious people, which is what we are in the Caribbean as well. Once again, I am forcing the parallel of a kind of mythology that coincides with the landscape.

So, to get back to the idea of Romare's imagery from the *Odyssey*: besides its veracity, there is the color, like the green surrounding that black figure going down through the water, which is absolutely, perfectly, the color of coral water, while the figure could simply be a coral diver or a shell diver going down to pick up shells from the bottom of the sea.[1] So this combination of images—the black diving figure and the green water—immediately strikes me not as Aegean but as completely Caribbean. And, as it is for Romare, it is perfectly valid for me to think of an archipelago in which there are boats and pigs and men, scared people and a succession of islands—home to me—to think of the *Odyssey* in terms of the Caribbean.

QUESTION: Well, you just made me think of *Another Life* and Captain Foquarde, who has pigs on his ship and is traveling around St. Lucia, and who also has a wife, Penelope, or a Penelope.[2]

DEREK WALCOTT: Yes, well, since Homer everybody is Odysseus or Penelope. Captain Ahab, for instance. It's just such a great story that everything multiplies off of it. A great poet like Joyce just said, yeah, it's one story—and I'll tell it again!

QUESTION: If you say that, for Helen, history is unimportant, what is the difference between Helen and Achille, who goes through this whole dream sequence in order to recover his history,[3] and why, then, is his version of history different from Helen's?

DEREK WALCOTT: Right, but he doesn't make himself go through that search. It's not a self-imposed thing. He's not an artist or a historian who imposes a duty on himself to do that, to write a book. The ideal thing—and I'm going to come back to the essence of the question—would be for the historian to say, "I'm Plunkett, and I'm going to say to this beautiful Black woman from St. Lucia, 'Oh, here's a book I wrote about you.'" She would say, "Oh, yeah? That's nice," and then promptly put the book aside. So what happened to her? Is that woman ignorant? No, she was beautiful *before* I wrote the book, and she will continue to be beautiful. She may appear to some to be stupid, illiterate, and backward, but not to me. She's saving it for history! This negligence that says, "Okay, great, but I don't care about a book about me, I don't care about a history about me"—this, to me, is essentially Caribbean not in the sense of ignorance or illiteracy, but rather in the sense of history and in the sense of art. It is no different from what we find in [Aimé] Césaire. When Césaire says, "Hooray for those who have invented nothing,"[4] you get the "bell curve" reaction. You know, "What have you guys done recently?"

"Well, we're trying to write some music here! Ah, but we're having some trouble catching up with you guys."

That is crap, okay? What Césaire says about the Caribbean is said by Pablo Neruda, and it is said in a different way by St. John Perse. The Caribbean writer wakes up every morning to a sense of complete erasure. There is no continuity. There is nothing to look at to confirm time. What does that mean? It concerns the ideology of the Western world, in terms of its arrogance, in terms of its conception of time. Except that great poets like Horace, like Shakespeare, say to you repeatedly, it doesn't matter about your monuments, it doesn't really matter, you know? You may not believe it, but Carthage can go; and if you want, Atlantis can go; Alexandria can go, but this little poem might last. It's true; it has happened. So it's not the vanity of art that says that; it's the reality of Western arrogance, of the presumption of permanence on the part of certain cultures, which great poets have written about in terms of a kind of erasure.

But getting back to Achille, the journey he makes is supposed to take place in an instant, during a moment of sunstroke which is magnified in time. It is true that in our dreams we have no idea of time. None. So what is a second? We don't know how long our dreams last, although scientists can now measure their duration. Time does not apply to the concept of a dream, so what happens to Achille in two seconds of total sunstroke or of dreaming can encompass centuries.

One of the greatest images in the history of literature is Dante's image of Neptune lying on the bottom of the sea, with the shadow of the *Argo* passing over him—that is just astonishing! That's the kind of thing Dante does for you—if you like jumping off a very high building! {*laughter*} But what he's saying is that time is of no consequence here. Imagine this image of Neptune at the bottom of the sea—Neptune being the sea. (You see, the danger of personification is that when we say "Neptune" we tend to think, "Oh, there's Neptune," a guy with a long beard, lying on his back.) To think of this myth in which Neptune is said to look up from where he is and to see the underside of the hull, the glimmering shadow of the *Argo* going across—that's the concept of time. It's astonishing; you gasp at this image of time. For Achille, the journey is back in time, to find out his name, and so he encounters his father, who has a particular name. (I took the father's name, "Afolabe," from a Nigerian actor and playwright, as a kind of homage to him.) When Afolabe asks Achille, "What do they call you?" he answers, "Achille." And when Afolabe says, "What does the name mean?" he replies, "I do not know."[5] You have to imagine a culture in which "Joe," say, would have a meaning. What does "Joe" mean? Joe? Joe means Joe! There are cultures that would ask, "What is Joe? What is a Joe? What is the meaning of that sound?" For somebody not to know the meaning of the sound of his or her name is to be nameless, not to have an identity. These are cultures in which the meaning of names is just absolutely crucial. What has been the experience in this part of the world of losing your name, of changing your name? You know that when you get to Ellis Island, you want to be American, you want to change your name from whatever to whatever—a kind of homogenized naming happens. So when Achille encounters his ancestor, who doesn't know what his name means, and the rage of the older man, who tells him that if he doesn't know what his name means, he doesn't exist, then there's a big crisis. Because he *does* exist, and he does have a name, yet he doesn't know the name he has been given, or what it means to be "Achille."

In the village in St. Lucia where I lived, or rather close to it, there was a man who ran a shop called "Hector's." And all the children in St. Lucia still sing the song "Helen of the West Indies," which is what the island is called because of its beauty and because it was fought over, changing hands twelve to thirteen times between the French and the British. St. Lucia was considered one of the most strategically important possessions because of its location, so it was fortified with a lot of tunnels and forts. At one point St. Lucia was offered in exchange for Canada. They made a mistake, and they took Canada. {*laughter*} But the shopkeeper named

Hector—this is true—had a cousin called Achille. Somebody in St. Lucia must have decided to call one child Hector and the other child Achille. Obviously, that's what happened. If you asked Hector what Hector did, he wouldn't know; if you asked Achille what Achilles did, he wouldn't know either. But if you look at someone with a magnificent physique, the kind of person you see all the time in St. Lucia (except they don't take care of their teeth, and that's sad; they can't afford to go to a dentist and their diet doesn't help)—if you look at those men working (and some of them have been used in films for this very reason), their bodies are in great shape. They are great-looking athletes, so you can easily say of any one of those men, look, there's Achilles, or, this guy looks like Hector. Why do you have to have that name? It's just that, if they are on a beach in the morning, running, then you think, hey, wait a minute! Subliminally, because of the great poem, you see these people as personifying it in some way. And there are many more associations of this kind.

So the book is really not about a model of another poem; it is really about associations, or references, because that is what we are in the Americas: we are a culture of references, not of certainties. There are no certainties in America. Walt Whitman knew that early on. He just said that there were no certainties, but only "I," meaning "the American," and meaning "Walt Whitman: I"; not "Walt Whitman, me Tarzan," but "Walt Whitman: I embody a new way of feeling." And when he says [to the Muse], "Cross out please those immensely overpaid accounts" from America, he doesn't mean that some people will become super-Americans (i.e., forget Europe, forget Greece, because we're Americans).[6] That's not what he's saying. He's saying—you have to read Whitman very, very carefully—"overpaid accounts." They've been paid over and over, the debts to Greece and Rome, et cetera. This is America—that forgetting, which has to be deliberate and must not be irresponsible. And then you see the vanity of this culture, America, that really believes in a lot of things. It believes, for instance, that it invented breathing. {*laughter*} The American poet believes that nobody in the history of the world breathed properly until 1926, or until scansion was discovered by certain U.S. poets who said, "The human breath consists of a trisyllabic stress." Now—I'm serious!—if you talk about people who are followers of William Carlos Williams, or somebody who says, "The human breath really consists of a very, very long inhalation and expulsion," you end up as a consequence with the Black Mountain school of breathing. Then you also have the school of asthmatic breathing, which is three beats to the line. This is very much like a dog panting, or something similar. {*laughter*}

What remains in the Caribbean, and in Caribbean fiction, is the human element of telling a story. The human ear, the human mind, the human audience cannot help but be dominated by its sense of time. And time is a clock ticking in a certain direction for a certain reason. Not all the geniuses of the world who believe that to be ridiculous can ever erase the basic need for narration. So in cultures like ours, which are still—in the opinion of some—young, things may be retained that another culture has lost. I think that contemporary culture has absolutely lost the idea of narration, arguing now that you don't need it. You don't need narration in painting, you don't need narration in anything, really, because who wants to hear, she got up, she did that, cha-cha-cha, da-da-da? There is something far beyond that. What is it—*quién sabe?* I don't know. But we are not interested, for the moment. So the Caribbean novel still tells a story; the Caribbean poem functions like a kind of melody, et cetera, et cetera. The Caribbean theater talks about people. What can happen, though, is that one can be accused of all sorts of things. But the worst thing to be accused of, and the most irritating (it's not really irritating, it's amusing), is having come to a point of arrest, of stasis, to hear: "Oh, that's sort of nineteenth century; we've done that, you know, we've passed that. People don't tell stories anymore. . . ." There was so much astonishment in the reviews when *Omeros* came out— first of all, that it should be so long, you know? Well, it isn't really, to me, a long poem. It is a book that got where it got to; it's not conceptually a massive thing. Then there was the idea of my undertaking something they call an epic, which I don't call an epic; I call it a very intimate work. All of that was there, I think, in the astonishment at the idea of something happening in a part of the world where it really should not have, that it should really have come from another, perhaps more "developed" place. And yet I think it is this whole freshness of experience that made me feel that my references to Homer, and to all the other writers I was indebted to in the book, were perfectly valid. And I knew it would lead to a kind of academic acclaim that I'm not very happy about—"Oh, so much is owed to so-and-so"—I hate that. It is a patronizing way of saying about, for instance, Romare's work: "Look at those black cutouts. They are like Greek vases." Yes, they may be like Greek vases, but they are *simultaneous* concepts, not *chronological* concepts. The black cutout of a diving figure is no more historical than the silhouette of a Greek athlete on a vase. It's not a question of where you stop, since you then have to go from the Greek silhouette back to the Egyptian profile, et cetera. If you think of art merely in terms of chronology, you are going to be patronizing to certain cultures. But if you think of art as a simultaneity that is inevitable in terms of certain people, then Joyce is a contemporary of Homer (which Joyce knew).

QUESTION: Picking up on some things you were just saying and what you said yesterday, if you're saying that Caribbean poetry, or rather your book, is a work of references, then these are references, as you pointed out yourself, that are lost on large parts of the Caribbean audience or on other people who might read your book—and I'd like to connect that with two things from yesterday. First of all, you raised the question of why write poetry, and that to me implies the related questions of why read poems and of who reads your poems, because it's obviously not—or, to a certain extent, can't be—the people you're writing about, who might not get the references. . . . And the second part of the question—

DEREK WALCOTT: Can I answer the first part? If you think of the proportion of people in America who read poetry {*laughter*}, we in the Caribbean may have a bigger proportion. In other words, if you have a population that totals, say, 100,000, and out of these, say, fifty people read poetry, that's a high proportion. I mean, in New York at a poetry reading at the Guggenheim that may draw 300, people are astonished at the size of the audience. "What an audience! Three hundred tonight!" And when some rock star has a concert, you can't get in! I'm not making that comparison invidiously, and I'm not putting down your question. What I'm saying is that there's no such thing, unfortunately, as writing for the common man. Now, maybe fifteen years ago, some Communist might have shot me for saying that, but no matter how much of an effort it is to do it, it's dangerous in this respect: it can be patronizing, obviously, and it can be insulting. The common man wants to get to *your* intelligence, and the thing to do is not to do that. And that includes, for me, the theater: If Shakespeare's attitude had been that he should write for the guys standing in the pit and talking, cursing, scratching, or whatever, then you would not have *Macbeth*. If he were writing for the common man, you would not expect to have that. You'd expect to have some inarticulate animal up there. But this does not mean that Shakespeare wrote for an elite. He always covered his you-know-what by writing another line that covered the big line. So he has, for example, this fantastic line: "the multitudinous seas incarnadine," and the guys are all going, wow, home run! The next line has four monosyllabic words out of five: "making the green one red." So some dummy in the front row goes, oh, yeah. {*laughter*} So you've got two intelligences, and each needs the other: "multitudinous seas incarnadine," which is just *incredible* (both visual and aural), followed by the other line, which compresses. It's also true in Dante, another great poet who produced a combination of the vulgar and the sublime, as you know. So in terms of writing in that way, I don't think I'm bothered about the reality of people not reading. One wishes they could, but the real danger is to pretend that one can write for the person in the street, in that sense. Second part of the question?

QUESTION: What do you expect a reader to get out of *Omeros*? Is it admiration for your art, or something else?

DEREK WALCOTT: This is a sincere thing to say, and it is also embarrassing to say because it is very intimate, very private: what I was trying to do was to express my gratitude for the island—for the people of the island, the beauty of the island. That was the first intention of the book. Now, it's not a thing you normally say in public, but I say it in all honesty today. You see, I really (this sounds so affected!) didn't care if the book was even reviewed. Not because I was above it, I just felt satisfied—but not in the sense of smugness. It didn't matter if nobody paid any attention to it. And when it began to happen, I felt a little bit, just a little bit violated, in terms of the privacy that existed between me and the island. (That's a very crappy thing to say, but it's true.) Then it began to manifest itself as a work that had to be looked at, especially with all the references to Homer, and people began to define me as someone who was a Greek scholar. You know, none of those references is "right"! They're all jumbled up. What I'm saying is that this free-form choice that is typical of work out there, which owes to everything and is referential in that sense, is very American, broadly speaking. And therefore to have Philoctete as a character, although Philoctetes is not, as far as I remember, a major character in the *Odyssey*, is to have a play by Sophocles jamming with a poem by Homer. It's not wrong in terms of the associations, however, because every new mythology has screwed up the one preceding it, gotten it wrong, including Christianity. They got it wrong—and then they started something! It's true of Rastafarianism. It's a metaphorical thing: all myth is metaphorical in that respect—it takes what it wants from different mythologies. An Egyptian god then becomes somebody else, with all the wrong attributes of that particular god. An Egyptian would say to a Greek, "No, you've got it wrong; he doesn't do that," and the Greek would reply, "Yeah, man, well we say he does." All mythology is belligerent. Rastafarians, for instance, believe—I think it's diminished now because of certain realities—in the sanctity of Haile Selassie. What is Rastafarian mythology based on? It's based on Exodus, on the Promised Land, on the condemnation of Babylon, and it's all a mélange. But, then, what religion is not a mélange? What culture is not a mélange? In that sense, then, the first impulse of the referential—what I have called the free-form choice—is not to verify the sources, but to accept the references, however "wrong" they may be. And that to me is very "New World."

QUESTION: You talk about poetry elsewhere as currency you can pass back and forth. Did you consider *Omeros* almost something like that—that there would be lines in it that people would hang onto? When you talk about God, for example? I mean, those are the things that people can hang onto, in the sense that they're meaningful; they address issues that people are concerned about.

DEREK WALCOTT: Certainly. I'm not pretending that that is all, but this is so very private and very touchy; I really can't talk about it too much. I'm just saying that if you know where I'm from, and the people I love—to write about them is not to write in the sense of "one day you will comprehend $x$ or $y$," or "you don't understand what I'm doing." I'm overwhelmed when I'm there on the island with them, and I get tremendous respect and love from them. So, I daresay, yes, there is a spiritual purpose—if you want to call it that—in my poem. The difference, I would think (and the reason why I don't like the idea of its being called an epic), is that a particular epic, any epic, has a kind of political destiny—conspicuously in an epic like *Idylls of the King*, in which Tennyson is saying, now listen, you people have been as great as some of those Roman guys, and here's what I'm doing to prove it. Then he goes on to use Arthurian legend to elevate the myth into great poetry. That's a kind of onerous responsibility, an almost municipal responsibility, rather than a source of inspiration. Or take Virgil's epic, where you get the founding of Rome in terms of "Aeneas does this, and you Romans, $x$ or $y$." That's manifest destiny. In a sense, it's even there in Whitman, as the future of America, et cetera, et cetera. Not explicitly, not in terms of political conquest, although he doesn't say a lot about the Indians, does Mr. Whitman. You have to leave that part of the story out.

So in relation to *Omeros*, you couldn't say that I've written an epic on this guy, Achille, who goes out to—I don't know what he's going to do!—all he can really do is fish. Yes, but then you see, a natural element is more challenging than an army. You can perhaps face an army. You cannot face a hurricane. And that's more epical.

QUESTION: What was *Omeros* before it became a 325-page poem? There must have been many stages.

DEREK WALCOTT: You're asking me how it started. The answers are very technical, and in that sense very boring. I remember writing some lines about—I didn't know who the person was, but I knew there was a figure on a beach who had left society, and I thought this must be Timon of Athens—who was this person? I remember writing some couplets about this figure and wondering why I was doing it; then, where we were staying in St. Lucia once, there was a rain, a phenomenal amount of rain. Days of it, like the rain in *One Hundred Years of Solitude*. And I thought, this has got to stop. It didn't stop. Quite terrifying, tropical rain. And just below us was a pig farm, and you could hear the pigs at night. So I went down to the pigs and interviewed them—asked them if they had ever heard of Circe {*laughter*}, and they said no! Anyway, that was then. Later, a friend of mine died, a very good actor, and I remember being in St. Lucia and writing a poem about seeing him in the hotel room, and that also seemed to be part of it. And I was in St. Thomas once when Romare was too, and I did a long poem about something. So all these things were beginning to feed into something. And then (I forget how) I came across a rhythm, a metrical rhythm, and the terza rima combined with it—and I thought, well! If there's poetic homage in the book, it's obviously homage to two forms: my rough hexameter, which is in Homer, and my rough terza rima, which is in Dante. So personally and subliminally, I acknowledge the presence that *any* person writing in this part of the world, in this language, would feel— every writer's debt to Dante and Homer, every *poet*'s debt to Dante. They are just two *massive* realities. To pretend to ignore them would be like saying that Mt. Kilimanjaro does not exist. So that kind of votive tribute feels perfectly appropriate to me.

QUESTION: Speaking of tributes, can I ask you about the vernacular? When I was rereading *Omeros* the other day, I was really struck again by the first line. You really commence with an example of the vernacular—

DEREK WALCOTT: That question is actually a cultural commercial! {*laughter*}

I will tell you what I mean by that. At one point I thought: Why aren't you doing this book in French Creole? For one or two reasons. French Creole, as a written language, drives me nuts. I hate the kind of thing some writers are doing now, which sounds like Tarzan talk, because basically Creole is French and has much more subtlety than it's given, in terms of what's written. So I didn't want to write that sort of thing. Then, as I began to try it in my own way, a very curious thing happened. I began to feel false. (This is *my* language, a language I can talk, which I do speak and enjoy speaking.) Then I got to a point where I said, no, you know, you're forcing this thing. It's not like you're saying, with Dante in the *De Vulgari Eloquentia*, there's Latin, and then there's Italian, and I'm going to write this in Italian. And you get to a point where you're doing the Italian and you say to yourself, come on, come on, now really! Quite apart from the work that that involves and the effort of making it happen, a political question can come up. You can ask yourself at that point, for instance, about the West, and about the Irish, and about national languages in general. At what point does this literary use of the vernacular become forced? Joyce, for one, had a very funny attitude toward Gaelic, right? Joyce realized, I think, that the inevitable direction of the Irish language was going to be toward English. And he had made his own language in *Finnegans Wake* by that time. (So that's Joyce: he invented his own language! Okay.) But there is a point at which this issue comes up in many different countries. It comes up in Ireland, it comes up in Wales, where the language is confronted by a political decision, and then what happens? Is the language going to go under because of the politics? Can you force a language on a people, in schools, et cetera? When does the vernacular become defensive? When does it become aggressive? And from my own experience, it was becoming an act of aggression for me to have to write it, quite apart from who could read it and who could translate it, for it would have to be translated. Why would I give myself the problem of translating something that I wasn't feeling very happy about? Then I thought, yeah, but there's another way—you could write the same thing in dialect. For me, however, to be honest about my tone—my interior tone, then and now—I do not think in dialect. I can't pretend that I do. I think in a certain tone, but that is not my language. Why should I be false to my interior rhythm for the sake of any other country, politics, or attitude toward language? So I hope I am true, tonally, to what I am writing. The same thing applies to other writers in different situations—Dylan Thomas, say, or Seamus Heaney—tonally, they are Welsh; tonally, they are

Irish. So the ideal inflection for Dylan Thomas is his own inflection, as it is for Seamus Heaney, or as it is for me, when I am reading something by me. The thing about these other languages is that the culture would consider it okay to put on an English accent if you were reading Tennyson, say, or Keats. Now Keats spoke in a terrible Cockney accent—we know that! So we know that if Keats gave a reading on the radio, he would go {*exaggerated Cockney accent*}: "Thou still unravish'd bride of quietness," and you would say, "Who the fuck is that?" And it would be John Keats, reading his own work, instead of the BBC {*affected BBC accent*}: "Thou still unravish'd bride of quietness." {*laughter*} Give it to John Keats {*Cockney impression repeated*}—because it's richer, since it's possible that Keats could have written *only* that way *because* of his Cockney-from-Hampstead accent.

So that had to go. And then I thought, well, if it's going to begin this way, to continue this way will lead to a crisis—if I made this vernacular and had a man talking this way, then there would be this work in English by somebody with some reputation, who would be read, and it would have people saying {*broad Creole accent*}: "This is how, one sunrise, we cut down them canoes."⁷ How can you do that? There are people at Oxford, or Harvard maybe, who are going to have to read this thing {*line repeated in broad Creole accent*}. And then I said, yes, that's how it has to be—but the Empire doesn't give in that easily! {*laughter*}

—Edited by Gregson Davis

### Notes

*Ed.'s note:* I have supplied the title and endnotes, as well as all bracketed text added for clarification or smoother transitions. Derek Walcott gave this talk at Duke University on 19 April 1995. The transcript was made by Carolyn Gerber from a taped recording in December 1996.

1   Walcott was again pointing at a Bearden collage in which two figures are depicted floating under the sea, a naked woman approaching a man around whose body a white cloth swirls. The collage may illustrate a scene from the episode in which the sea-nymph Ino–Melicertes rescues Odysseus.

2   See "The Divided Child," in *Another Life* (New York, 1973), esp. 39–40.

3   See *Omeros* (New York, 1990), 133–51 (3.25–28).

4   See Aimé Césaire, *Cahier d'un retour au pays natal*, 2d ed. (Paris, 1956), 71.

5   *Omeros*, 137 (3.25.3).

6   See Walt Whitman, "Song of the Exposition," in *Leaves of Grass*, ed. Emory Holloway (Garden City, 1926 [1891]), 165–73, esp. 165.

7   The opening line of *Omeros*.

**Joseph Farrell**

Walcott's *Omeros*: The Classical Epic
in a Postmodern World

Let me begin with an anecdote. I have a
daughter who is a student in the Philadelphia
public school system. Like any other big-city
school system, ours has its problems, but so
far they have seemed manageable. If nothing
else, trying to negotiate the school-district bu-
reaucracy provides parents with a rich store of
strange experiences that we enjoy sharing with
one another. This particular story concerns race.
Again like most cities, Philadelphia has had to
cope with the problem of segregation by race,
which it has chosen to address in the schools
not by busing but by a voluntary desegregation
program. Schools in the "deseg" program receive extra funding from the central district and
consequently have more instructional and sup-
port staff, enrichment programs, and so forth.
Parents choose whether to participate in the program and designate, in order of preference, the
schools they would like their child to attend. The
children are selected by lottery and assigned to
a school on the basis of their number and their
race: almost everything depends on whether the
school you want your child to attend needs more

The *South Atlantic Quarterly* 96:2, Spring 1997.
Excerpted from Margaret Beissinger et al., eds., *Epics and the
Contemporary World*, forthcoming from, and published with
the permission of, University of California Press.

White, Black, Asian, or Hispanic children in that particular year. The year we applied marked the first time that the aspirations of anyone in our family had so explicitly been tied to his or her race.

My daughter's name is Flannery—not the most common name—and when a child who bears it encounters another Flannery, it creates a special bond. One of the Flannerys we know is further distinguished by the fact that she is a twin and that she and her brother, Schuyler, have one White and one Black parent. It is their experience with the deseg system, a parental war story, that I want to recount. Because race is the only criterion for admitting a child to a deseg school, the district requires interested parents to specify their child's race and to do so in terms that are literally black and white: they recognize nothing in between. Flannery and Schuyler's parents balked at this. To identify their children as either Black or White would go against everything they stand for, both in their marriage and in terms of the absolutely interracial identity that they cherish in their children. But a choice had to be made. When they simply refused, the bureaucrat in charge of the interview, who had no doubt been through this before, sighed wearily and said, "Well, I guess we're just going to have to subject them to the eyeball test." The parents were too astonished to protest before the children were sized up by the bureaucrat, whose job at that moment was simply to determine their race by his own judgment about the color of their skin. And in a decision that could have been scripted by Solomon, but more likely by Kafka, he found that one of the twins was Black and the other White.

Derek Walcott has been subjected repeatedly to the literary-critical equivalent of this test and indeed invites such scrutiny by the way in which he thematizes his own racially mixed ancestry.[1] As he wrote over thirty years ago in the often-quoted poem "A Far Cry from Africa,"

> I who am poisoned with the blood of both,
> Where shall I turn, divided to the vein?
> I who have cursed
> The drunken officer of British rule, how choose
> Between this Africa and the English tongue I love?
> Betray them both, or give back what they give?
> How can I face such slaughter and be cool?
> How can I turn from Africa and live?[2]

Years later, in "The Hotel Normandie Pool," the theme returns:

> And I, whose ancestors were slave and Roman,
> have seen both sides of the imperial foam,
> heard palm and pine tree alternate applause
> as the white breakers rose in galleries
> to settle, whispering at the tilted palm
> of the boy-god Augustus. My own face
> held negro Neros, chalk Caligulas;
> my own reflection slid along the glass
> of faces foaming past triumphal cars.[3]

The motif of racial indeterminacy presents itself throughout Walcott's poetry in other registers as well, such as the linguistic register, in which English threatens to occlude the Creole dialects of St. Lucia; the literary-historical register, in which Walcott speculates on his own storyteller's craft in relation to that of the Caribbean "man of words" and of Shakespeare, to name but two of his many models; the religious register, in which St. Lucia's Catholic culture contrasts with Walcott's own Methodist upbringing, while both Christian traditions maintain a dialogue with the folk religion of the common people and with the animism of the island's ancient inhabitants; among many other registers, including the one on which I will focus: the generic register. For the debate (if I may call it that) over the genre of *Omeros* shares with the questions posed in these other registers the twin motifs of dichotomy and indeterminacy, both of which cast a strong and useful light on the poem and on the concept of genre itself.

Nevertheless, even characterizing discussion of the poem's genre as a debate is an overstatement. Diverging opinions there have been, but little dialogue. Classicists such as Mary Lefkowitz, Oliver Taplin, and Bernard Knox, as well as the Eurocentric comparatist George Steiner, have expressed little doubt about the poem's epic character.[4] But Sidney Burris, while hailing it as a "sprawling new poem" of "herculean ambition," pointedly avoids using the word "epic," calling *Omeros* a Caribbean "national *narrative*."[5] Similarly, longtime students of Walcott and of West Indian literature generally have been chary of the epic label. It is true that Robert Hamner, one of the world's foremost experts on Walcott, has not shied away from it.[6] But John Figueroa, perhaps the dean of West Indian literary studies and a former teacher of Walcott's, in what was probably the first scholarly commentary on the poem stated flatly and preemptively, "*Omeros* is not an epic."[7] Similarly, Patricia Ismond, another distinguished West Indianist and Walcott specialist, finds *Omeros* informed by a lyric rather than an epic sensibility.[8] Finally, I should mention that this is the tack taken by Walcott himself: "I do not think of it as an epic. Certainly not in the sense of epic design. Where are the battles? There are a few, I suppose. But 'epic' makes people think of great wars and great warriors. That isn't the Homer I was thinking of; I was thinking of Homer the poet of the seven seas."[9]

This last remark points to the different ways in which critics have viewed *Omeros*'s relationship to the *Iliad* and the *Odyssey*. Eurocentric critics have been quick to identify the poem's "debt" to Homer as its essential distinguishing characteristic; Taplin perhaps goes farthest in this regard.[10] Burris, in contrast, predicts that "commentators on *Omeros* . . . will understandably busy themselves in tracking down the Homeric parallels in Walcott's poem," but argues that this will be "a particularly ill-fated approach because part of the poem's task, its attempt to recreate the original authenticity of Walcott's Caribbean culture, lies in its deliberate deflation of analogy."[11] The most important antecedents of *Omeros*, Burris suggests, are to be found in Walcott's own dramatic works and in another quasi-Homeric work of great generic indeterminacy, Joyce's *Ulysses*.[12] Figueroa goes even farther, stating that "Walcott's poem is not an imitation of either the *Iliad* or the *Odyssey*. . . . The point of the use of Homer lies elsewhere," notably, in his metaphorical or allegorical significance "as the great creator," especially of poetic language, "as the Blind Seer," a wanderer held in no great honor whose suffering has gained him an acute understanding of the nature of things, and even as a kind of poetic savior who rescues Walcott's Narrator from the sins that have beset other poets.[13] But this Homer is, finally, a symbol of "the foreign in West Indian culture, especially . . . the non-African foreign," an element that is itself in need of redemption: for Figueroa, the question of the value of a poem like *Omeros* has less to do with "what influences are at play"—with whether the poem merits a place in the apostolic succession of Homeric imitators—than with "the quality of what is made" out of such influences, whether they bear the authentic stamp of Homeric originality.[14]

There has thus been considerable anxiety among critics and on the part of the poet himself about the generic affinities of *Omeros*. One may conjecture that many of those who hail the poem as an epic do so without much interest in genre theory, but from a desire to honor Walcott for what is indeed a remarkable achievement. Most critics appear to regard the entire issue of genre as unfortunate, any choice among the available categories being difficult, if not impossible, for readers to make. Despite the difficulty, however, critics raise the issue as one that is somehow necessary to confront, even if some can manage only an equivocal resolution like that of the reviewer who described the poem as, "if anything," a novel in verse.[15]

Any uncertainty raised by the epic pretensions of *Omeros* stems from the obvious fact that the poem does not conform rigidly to the generic expectations most readers bring to classical European epic poetry. In a way, this attitude is preferable to its opposite, with *Omeros* regarded unproblematically as an epic in the Homeric tradition. The poem is, without question, about problems of belonging, concerning itself with the dubious prospect that any of us might find real comfort in a sense of belonging to some putatively homogeneous group. The problem of literary categorization is thus merely a special case of one of the poem's central themes; but it gains point from the fact that epic—particularly European epic in the classical tradition—has been perceived as (to use Bakhtin's term) the "monologic" genre par excellence and as the antithesis of the most thoroughly open and dialogic genre, which Bakhtin terms the novel.[16]

When it comes to the assessment of postcolonial literature, the critical discourse of epic poetry acquires a racist tinge. Ultimately, I believe, it is the notion that the European epic speaks with the voice of the accumulated authority of generations of White imperialist culture that leads many readers to deny *Omeros* any meaningful association with the epic genre, while in the open polyphony of novelistic genres they find a quality better suited to the creolization of language, the racial and literary miscegenation, that characterizes the poem. The debate clearly goes far beyond mere taxonomy and becomes a political battle for Walcott's racial identity and ethnic soul: Is the author of *Omeros* "really" the White Walcott descended in blood from men of Warwickshire and in ink from the Bard of Avon, or is he the Black descendant of slaves whose history and language have all but disappeared from the official record, a man whose story can be told only in novelistic opposition to the epic culture that seeks to co-opt him as its own spokesman? In this light, it becomes clear that the epic element in *Omeros* threatens to reopen an old debate over Walcott's relationship to the European and African elements in his personal heritage and in the culture of the West Indies as a whole.[17]

My response to those critics who feel compelled to deny that *Omeros* is an epic poem is twofold: first, to base such a denial on a desire to claim *Omeros* as an *Afro*-Caribbean poem ignores those contemporary studies in world epic that go well beyond the literary tradition defined by European poets such as Homer and Milton; second, to distinguish *Omeros* from its predecessors in the canonical epic tradition on the basis of its capacity to celebrate alterity ignores the European epic's capacity for self-questioning and for radical reinterpretation of its own generic roots. Let me expand upon both points.

Those critics who are embarrassed by the possibility that *Omeros* might be taken for an epic, hence a White man's poem, are (no doubt unknowingly) endorsing an untenable and extremely reactionary view of what epic poetry is in its racial and world-cultural dimensions. Such a view, to be sure, has been maintained by a number of "authoritative" discussions of epic as a world genre; but these discussions are easily shown to be deeply, if unwittingly, implicated in a racist discourse of shocking naiveté.

The idea that African nations were actually incapable of producing an epic literature was articulated, perhaps not for the first time but with embarrassing clarity, by Sir Maurice Bowra in his 1952 study *Heroic Poetry*. In surveying the heroic poetry of a wide variety of world literatures, Bowra noted the close relationships between poetry of praise or of lamentation and the heroic poetry with which he was concerned, but observed that the first two categories "exist in some societies where heroic poetry is lacking," a lack he ascribed to an "inability to rise beyond a single occasion to the conception of a detached art." Citing examples from Africa—specifically, from Uganda and Ethiopia—he concluded that "though these poems, and many others like them, show a real admiration for active and generous manhood, they come from peoples who have no heroic poetry and have never advanced beyond panegyric and lament. The intellectual effort required for such an advance seems to have been beyond their powers." It is depressing to observe how often these and similarly demeaning cultural stereotypes leap to Bowra's mind as he discusses the literary achievements of African peoples. Characteristic is his assumption that heroic verse represents a later and more developed stage of the panegyric and lament found in Africa, the idea that a literary culture must progress from these early stages toward a true heroic literature and that heroic poetry calls for a degree of intellectual abstraction of which Africans are not, in his view, capable; rather, the poetry that they do produce is notable for its "simple and primitive" qualities, its "expression of an immediate and violent excitement."[18]

Bowra's views, which strike us today as ignorant and insulting, are fully representative of literary scholarship in his day, and he was far from alone in believing that epic was simply not an African genre. A similar opinion was voiced in 1970, this time on purely formal grounds rather than as a judgment on the intellectual capacities of the African artist, by the influential folklorist Ruth Finnegan.[19] But by then the tide had begun to turn, and considerable work has been done by now both to make the existence of an epic literature among a number of African peoples known and to study its particular qualities.

The procedure followed by many studies of the African epic is double: scholars such as Isidore Okpewho and John William Johnson aim to show, on the one hand, that the African epic is recognizable as epic in the same terms as canonical European specimens and, on the other, that it displays certain distinctive characteristics as a primarily oral and performative, rather than literary, genre.[20] For this reason Africanists have an important role to play, first and self-evidently in the comparative study of oral epic as a phenomenon of world literature, but also, to the extent that research into oral poetry has revolutionized the study of the Homeric poems, in the effort to reinterpret the canonical tradition of European epic that boasts of its Homeric ancestry. One consequence of this activity is that African epic has been subjected to some of the same questions that had begun to be asked of both archaic Greek epic and its putative modern European analogues, principally, the South Slavic epic poetry recorded and studied by Milman Parry and Albert Lord.[21] It can now be seen that the African material stands in more or less the same relation as the Slavic material to texts like the Homeric *Iliad* and *Odyssey*, even if one concludes that the Homeric poems are by comparison only vestigially oral performances that traveled some considerable way before reaching literary fixedness. For instance, in order to illustrate oral poetry's tendency to strive for immediate effect by means of humor, Okpewho compares the grim humor shown by the narrator of the *Kambili* epic ("The old sandle man's head was cut off at his neck. / Big trouble has begun in Jimini! / The little man fell flopping about like a tramp in the cold"[22]) to Patroclus's ill-timed and entirely out-of-character jeering at the Trojan Cebriones, whom he has just killed. But it is clear that what Okpewho regards as a typical and even normative procedure for the Mandingo poet is present, though comparatively rare, in the Homeric poems.[23] If we are unconvinced by this particular analogy, however, other examples come to mind: the Homeric narrator's ironic aside concerning the bargain struck by Glaucus, who exchanges his golden armor for Diomedes' bronze (*Iliad* 6.234–36);[24] or perhaps Odysseus's observation to his host and principal listener, Alcinous, that his story is getting rather long and it might be time simply to stop and go to bed (*Odyssey* 11.328–84). This exchange occurs about halfway through the hero's narrative of his adventures since the Trojan War and, not incidentally, about halfway through the poem as a whole. When Alcinous refuses to hear of any delay in the completion of the tale, we may take his reaction as the oral poet's script for his ideal audience, who should be as eager for the rest of his story as Alcinous is for that of Odysseus.[25]

Passages like these are admittedly not very common in our *Iliad* and *Odyssey*, or perhaps they tend to be overlooked by readers unaccustomed to finding such elements in epics of the European canon. But despite Homer's distance from actual oral performance, comparative studies have established the ultimately oral and performative character of Homeric epic, thus aligning the *Iliad* and the *Odyssey* with modern world epic, as opposed to the remainder of the ancient, medieval, and early modern tradition of "classicizing" European epic in the Homeric tradition—the *Aeneid*, for instance, or *La Divina Commedia*, *Os Lusíadas*, *Paradise Lost*, and so forth. This is a crucial point because the scholarly discovery of an African epic linked to Homer by virtue of its being the product of an oral-epic performance culture actually parallels one of the dominant conceits of literary apologia in *Omeros*—namely, Walcott's construction of Homer not as a participant in an exclusively European scribal culture but as a singer of folktales whom one might find just as readily in an African or Afro-Caribbean context as in that of archaic Greece.

For Walcott, the Creole culture of the Caribbean is preeminently an oral culture. In "Cul de Sac Valley" he contrasts this culture with the scribal one in which he works, calling Creole "a tongue they speak / in, but cannot write." He imagines himself as a poet/carpenter creating a work that perfectly images his Caribbean homeland:

> as consonants scroll
> off my shaving plane
> in the fragrant Creole
> of their native grain;
>
> from a trestle bench
> they'd curl at my foot,
> C's, R's, with a French
> or West African root
>
> from a dialect throng-
> ing, its leaves unread
> yet light on the tongue
> of their native road.[26]

But as he catches the fresh scent from a stand of trees in the landscape he wishes to represent—trees designated in French Creole as *bois canot, bois campêche*—his dream of honestly representing that landscape is shattered as he imagines the trees "hissing" at him with reproach:

> . . . *What you wish*
> *from us will never be,*
> *your words is English,*
> *is a different tree.*[27]

Here the poet's language and his status as a member of the scribal culture distance him from the oral culture of his Creole home.

The motif of Caribbean culture as grounded in orality is basic to Walcott's thinking on language. His play *O Babylon!* concerns the cultural and political ideals of a Rastafarian community in Kingston, Jamaica. In a note on the play, Walcott writes of the Jamaican spoken dialect in its pure form as unintelligible except to Jamaicans and thus in need of translation to any outsider; and "within that language . . . the Rastafari have created still another for their own nation . . . have invented a grammar and a syntax which immure them from the seductions of Babylon, an oral poetry which requires translation into the language of the oppressor. To translate is to betray."[28] This confession pertains in the first instance to the author's project of representing an oral culture in a scripted play; but it sheds a painful light on his effort to write a West Indian poetry at all, particularly to write it in English. Such an effort must be fatally flawed from the start because any English poem, any written work, stands at an extra degree of separation from its subject as compared with Creole utterance. It possesses the quality not so much of an original composition as of a translation— and, thus, of a betrayal.

What is crucial, however, is one's response to the recognition of this betrayal. If there is a *division* between English and Creole, between scribal and oral cultures, between Europe and Africa, there is also a *relationship* to be negotiated. It is this insight that makes a place for the craft of translation, a space that is inevitably, necessarily *there*. Translation is, however, a transitive process: if Creole must be translated into English, the converse is also true. If European colonialists bring foreign categories of intellection to the interpretation of Caribbean realities, it is equally possible to translate European culture into West Indian terms; and while this latter type of translation is less common, given the asymmetrical power relationship between the European colonialists and the islanders, it shares with all forms of translation the impossibility of leaving the "original" unchanged. The decision to translate Homeric epic into West Indian terms cannot but change one's perception of Homer. Thus Walcott's characterization of Caribbean dialects as "oral poetry" is paralleled by his refusal to cede Homer to the scribal culture of the European colonialists.

This is no minor theme in *Omeros* (or, indeed, in Walcott's work as a whole) but a central problem to which the poem constantly and broodingly recurs. The theme is sounded first in the image of Seven Seas, a blind old man identified by the Narrator with Omeros (1.2.2–3). Seven Seas spends some of his days sitting in the No Pain Café, observed by its proprietor, Ma Kilman: "Sometimes he would sing. . . . // . . . But his words were not clear. / They were Greek to her. Or old African babble."[29] It is Seven Seas who, like a prophet, discloses to Philoctete the meaning of Achille's unusual overnight absence from port: he has journeyed to Africa in search of "his name and his soul."[30]

This equivalence between Greek and "old African babble" involves an approximation of Homer's oral poetry to elements in West Indian speech that must remain, even to many West Indian listeners, inarticulate and at best partially understood. This motif finds its parallel in other contexts, such as when, in the Narrator's interview with Homer himself, the ancient poet declares that "a drifter / is the hero of my book" and the Narrator surprises him by rejoining, "I never read it"—which he then qualifies—"not all the way through."[31] For the reader alive to the poem's engagement with its literary antecedents, it is a puzzling moment.[32] I take this reply as a rejection of what is implied when Homer refers to his *Odyssey* as a "book." Homer is not to be exclusively understood as the representative, nor *Omeros* as the product, of European scribal culture; for, after denying that he has ever "read" Homer "all the way through," the Narrator declares his debt to the oral tradition, going on to insist:

> . . . I have always heard
> your voice in that sea, master, it was the same song
> of the desert shaman, and when I was a boy
>
> your name was as wide as a bay, as I walked along
> the curled brow of the surf; the word "Homer" meant joy,
> joy in battle, in work, in death, then the numbered peace
>
> of the surf's benedictions, it rose in the cedars,
> in the *laurier-cannelles*, pages of rustling trees.
> Master, I was the freshest of all your readers.[33]

This emphasis on Homer as an oral poet of the sea and of nature, one whose poetry finds its analogue not in literature but in the unwritten landscape and seascape of St. Lucia, in the quotidian experience of a growing boy, constructs a Homer who is very different from his Vergilian and Miltonic progeny, one with a much closer resemblance to the Slavic and African epic poets recovered by folklorists. If this Homer can be encountered at all through reading, it can only be a partial encounter—"not all the way through"—for he is to be found not just in the leaves of a book but also in the "pages" of the "trees."[34]

In this respect research into the existence and oral-performative character of the African epic, and the establishment of a link between these traditions and those that produced the songs of Homer, substantiates Walcott's imaginative characterization of Homer, in one of many avatars within *Omeros*, as Seven Seas, the wizened old storyteller of St. Lucia who embodies the lore and wisdom of the island people and whose roots are ultimately in Africa.

My second main point concerns the way in which most students of literature have been taught to conceive of the European epic. It is clear that the study of world epic in the twentieth century represents a major challenge to traditional definitions of the genre based on the European canon. In addition, these traditional definitions are wholly inadequate to describe even such poems as the *Aeneid* and *Paradise Lost*. A good deal of the modern theoretical discourse that concerns itself with epic, notably, the classic formulations—descended from Schiller—of Hegel, Lukács, Auerbach, and Bakhtin, shows a pronounced tendency to employ a discursive caricature of the genre as a foil for the less strictly defined, formally and culturally heterogeneous, and "open" characteristics of other genres, especially the novel.[35]

This discursive strategy has resulted in a number of pernicious literary-historical misconceptions, not least of which is the absurdly one-dimensional idea of the epic genre that many students of literature regard as axiomatic. Thus while the epic, viewed from a multicultural perspective, may prove to be many things, in the classical tradition of European literature it has been accorded a privileged place as one of the most elevated genres. Among its attributes (along with a tone conforming to its elevated matter) are *authority*, or the idea that the stories told by the epic narrator are literally true; *transcendence*, or the idea that the authority and truth of epic narrative are wholly independent of any historical or cultural contingency; and *originality*, the idea that epic is in some sense a source or font of culture, particularly as the literary embodiment of a nation's character.

If we define the European epic as necessarily characterized by these attributes, it is easy to see why some readers would be hesitant to regard *Omeros* as representative of the genre. Its tone is seldom elevated, nor is much of its matter especially dignified. The narrative voice, though sure in a technical sense, is personal (in many passages explicitly autobiographical), uncertain (readier to ask questions than to provide answers), idiosyncratic (prone to seemingly uncontrolled punning), and uncomfortable with the mantle of authority. The narrative itself is often untrue in any conventional sense: the Narrator does not really speak with his dead father or with Homer; Achille does not really sail to his ancestral Africa; and Dennis Plunkett is neither the father nor the descendant of the obscure midshipman who bore the same surname and who died in the Battle of Les Saintes. It is also clear that the nationalism of this epic is far from embracing the imperialist ideology of previous epics, Walcott's St. Lucia being consistently represented as a remnant and a victim of empire. As one among many Caribbean islands, the formerly contested possession of rival empires now left to fend for itself seems both an unlikely subject for a triumphalist national epic and an unlikely heir to the epic tradition handed down from Greece, Rome, and Christendom in general.

If there were any doubt that *Omeros* is a deliberate non-epic, it would seem to be dispelled by a passage that occurs near the end of the poem, in which Walcott imagines what a conventional epic description of St. Lucia might have looked like:

> *In the mist of the sea there is a horned island*
> *with deep green harbours where the Greek ships anchor*
>
> *. . . .*
> *It was a place of light with luminous valleys*
>
> *under thunderous clouds. A Genoan wanderer*
> *saying the beads of the Antilles named the place*
> *for a blinded saint. Later, others would name her*
>
> *for a wild wife. Her mountains tinkle with springs*
> *among moss-bearded forests, and the screeching of birds*
> *stitches its tapestry. The white egret makes rings*
>
> *stalking its pools. African fishermen make boards*
> *from trees as tall as their gods with their echoing*
> *axes, and a volcano, stinking with sulphur,*
>
> *has made it a healing place.*[36]

The style of this passage, its beauty notwithstanding, might strike the reader as absurd and hence as sheerly parodic in the usually unpretentious linguistic context of *Omeros*, with its stretches of plain dialogue, its Creole, its occasional obscenities. But there is no mockery here. The passage is uttered first by Omeros himself, who observes the Narrator weeping like a boy:

> and he saw how deeply I had loved the island.
> Perhaps the oarsman knew this, but I didn't know.
> Then I saw the ebony of his lifted hand.

And Omeros nodded: "We will both praise it now."
But I could not before him. My tongue was a stone
at the bottom of the sea, my mouth a parted conch

from which nothing sounded, and then I heard his own
Greek calypso coming from the marble trunk,
widening the sea with a blind man's anger.[37]

Omeros sings the first two lines of the song quoted above, then the Narrator continues, "and the waves were swaying to the stroke of his hand, // as I heard my own thin voice riding on his praise / the way a swift follows a crest, leaving its shore." They sing the remaining stanzas together, until the Narrator informs us, "My voice was going / under the strength of his voice, which carried so far / that a black frigate heard it, steadying its wing."[38] The concentration of literary motifs in this passage—its elevated tone; the classical conceit marked by both Omeros and the Narrator being on a boat (i.e., composing poetry figured as sailing, the allusions to specific literary voyages such as that of Dante and Vergil across the Styx); Omeros's vatic knowledge of the Narrator's love, unsuspected by himself, for his native land; the response of the waves and the frigate bird to the Orphic power of Omeros's song; the blending of the poets' voices; and the younger poet's inability to sing before hearing the voice of the elder—all represent a departure from the "normal" (if one can speak of a norm) narrative style of the poem up to this point. Through this departure, and in the distance it takes us from the poem's usual stylistic procedures, we can measure the gap between *Omeros* and other epics of the Homeric stripe.

A second passage, occurring not long after this one, accomplishes something similar but in a less striking way. The poem's final chapter begins as follows:

I sang of quiet Achille, Afolabe's son,
who never ascended in an elevator,
who had no passport, since the horizon needs none,

never begged nor borrowed, was nobody's waiter,
whose end, when it comes, will be a death by water
(which is not for this book, which will remain unknown

and unread by him). I sang the only slaughter
that brought him delight, and that from necessity—
of fish, sang the channels of his back in the sun.

I sang our wide country, the Caribbean Sea.
Who hated shoes, whose soles were as cracked as a stone,
who was gentle with ropes, who had one suit alone,

whom no man dared insult and who insulted no one,
whose grin was a white breaker cresting, but whose frown
was a growing thunderhead, whose fist of iron

would do me a greater honour if it held on
to my casket's oarlocks than mine lifting his own
when both anchors are lowered in the one island.[39]

Such a passage is literally perverse, turned backwards, alluding in the poem's final chapter to the conventional opening of a canonical epic. Indeed, one can easily read the first line of the chapter as an allusion to the opening lines of the *Iliad*, but an allusion that systematically inverts virtually everything in its source: Μῆνιν ἄειδε, θεά, Πηληιάδεω Ἀχιλλῆος / οὐλομένην (Sing, goddess, the baleful anger of Peleus's son, Achilles). Every departure from the Homeric model speaks eloquently of the vast difference in perspective between the two poems. In naming his own hero, Walcott rejects the universal form "Achilles" in favor of the dialectal variant "Achille," local Creole by way of colonial French. By including the patronymic he underlines the theme of cultural rift; for while Achilles and Peleus share membership in a single Hellenic culture, the very names of Achille and Afolabe represent the victimization of Africans in the Americas at the hands of the European slave trade. The epithet "quiet" is, of course, unimaginable for any Homeric hero. Finally, in "I sang" two crucial reversals occur. First, in the change of tense and mood from Homer's forward-looking "sing" (ἄειδε) is figured the dislocation, as mentioned above, of the epic invocation from the poem's beginning to its end. Second, and more tellingly, Homer's "goddess" (θεά), the Muse, disappears: the poet, having no need to petition divinity for his song, mortal and fallible though he may be, sings on his own authority. For some readers it is this more than anything else that places *Omeros* outside the bounds of the epic genre. "*Omeros* is not an epic," writes John Figueroa, "and it hardly touches on the gods."[40] Indeed, it is in passages like this one that we squarely confront Sidney Burris's "deliberate deflation of analogy."

If the European epic is what the theorists tell us it should be, then clearly *Omeros* is no epic. But those theorists are wrong. Certainly, the idea that epic is a closed, authoritative genre, objective in its regard of the heroic past, and so on, is a significant discursive construct that evidently answers some deep-seated cultural longing on the part of readers brought up on European literature. But a discursive construct it is, and its usefulness in describing or understanding an actual epic poem is limited at best. The discourse on the epic is, to be sure, one of the longest-lived and most powerful elements of literary investigation in the West. The fact is, however, that there has always been a countertradition of reading epic as more open to pluralities of interpretation than the conventional view of the genre would seem to allow, and such interpretations have recently become a dominant feature of the critical discussion. From ancient allegoresis of the Homeric epics, which refused to take the poems at face value, to Romantic readings of Satan as the hero of *Paradise Lost*, to New Critical readings of the *Aeneid* as a deeply divided, grimly brooding meditation on the costs of empire, practical critics have always shown great acuity and resourcefulness at reading behind the objectivity and transcendence that we have all been taught to find in epic the cultural anxieties and historical contingencies reflected and refracted within what poses as the inevitability of epic narrative.[41] It is in general fair to say that the rigid conception of epic I have been outlining here is by and large the province of theorists, who find such a construct useful for their own discursive purposes, and of nonspecialists, who are by definition not very interested in the epic; the excellent work done by a number of connoisseurs, on the other hand, shows that an acceptance of alterity has been a basic constitutive feature of the European epic from its inception. To deny that *Omeros* is an epic on the grounds that it is something "other" than the *Iliad* or *Paradise Lost* is to misunderstand the development of European epic as badly as Bowra misunderstood the nature of African epic.

But even if *Omeros* does not conform to the expectations of theorists and nonspecialists, it does not fail to satisfy them. Walcott's ironic handling of the generic conventions of classical epic poetry is in my view more convincingly read as a logical extension of the genre's capacity to reinvent itself through inversion, opposition to epic predecessors, and ironic self-reflexion. To return briefly to the end of the poem: by announcing his subject here rather than at the beginning of the poem, the Narrator inverts normal epic procedure. While this particular stratagem is an innovation, I believe, it is of a piece with the kind of striving for novelty that one finds throughout post-Homeric epic. That is to say, it is precisely the kind of innovation, commonly identified with Greek poetry of the Hellenistic period but found everywhere in Vergil, Camões, and Milton as well, whereby either adherence to epic convention or imitation of a particular epic model is pointedly varied in such a way as to force rethinking about fundamental aspects of the genre.[42] This capacity for innovation has come to be seen as a central characteristic of both individual poets (e.g., Vergil's internal dialogue between the voices of celebration and lament, and his re- duction of the hero and his enemy to a single pattern) and the tradition as a whole (e.g., Milton's recasting of the classical pagan hero as a demon to be surpassed and defeated by a new Christian hero possessed of qualities dia- metrically opposed to those of his prototype and foe).[43] Indeed, two recent studies of the European epic argue convincingly that the genre can only be understood in dialectical terms. For David Quint, the dialectic takes shape over time, with each instantiation of epic narrative finding its place on a continuum that lies between a wholehearted commitment to the celebra- tion of triumph and a dissenting point of view that consistently takes the side of a defeated resistance. For Susanne Wofford, the epic poem is dia- lectical in its very structure, with the simile, the epic figure par excellence, being the means by which the genre attempts to correlate its heroic ideol- ogy with the (largely antithetical) values of the external world. Over time, Wofford argues, the genre has developed various strategies for negotiating this disjunctive relationship, which nevertheless remains apparent to the reader and plays an essential role in constituting the epic. Both Quint and Wofford thus present views of the epic that are profoundly at odds with received opinion concerning the closed, monologic nature of the genre; moreover, their ideas, while developed and expressed with great energy and uncommon insight, are by no means eccentric relative to the bulk of contemporary critical work on the European epic. Indeed, one might say that they represent an important stage in theoretical work on the epic and a signal that in this field theory has finally begun to catch up with practice.[44]

Thus the polyglossia of *Omeros* does not just flout epic convention or render allusion to the classical epics merely parodic or unimportant, but actually continues the epic tradition of the poet's questioning and self- questioning engagement with his predecessors. Placing at the end of the poem a passage that the "rules" of the genre tell us should come at the be- ginning is a formal instance of the capacity for inversion and reinvention that is itself a property of the epic genre. We may also take it as a signal that more substantive forms of inversion and reinvention are under way as well.

Once we realize this, it becomes clear that my earlier hypothetical argument, in which I adduced this passage to prove that *Omeros* is no epic, is itself open to drastic revision. To begin with, I called "Achille" a "dialectal variant" of "Achilles," the "universal" name for the greatest of heroes. This position is correct within the confines of a discourse that regards epic as the literary embodiment of a unitary, undifferentiated "European" culture, but a modest amount of philological inquiry reveals what is wrong with this perspective. "Achilles" happens to be the form that the name takes in English as well as in Latin, and it is through Latin that the form acquired its apparent universality. In fact, though, like "Ulysses" for "Odysseus" and "Hercules" for "Herakles," this form is a Roman corruption of the Greek "Akhilleus." In other words, it is itself a dialectal variant. It is clear that *Omeros* invites precisely this kind of scrutiny; consider its title, which designates the master poet of the tradition it engages not by the spuriously universal Latinate "Homer" (<Latin "Homerus") but by the Greek "Omeros." Indeed, even here we cannot claim a fixity or an authenticity that can pass for universality, for it is not the form that an ancient Greek would have used—"Ομηρος (i.e., HO-me-ros)—but is Modern Greek as spoken to the Narrator by a Greek woman and transcribed without regard for the conventions of the written language.[45] It is the sound of the word that captivates the Narrator, who supplies it with his own idiosyncratic, aural etymology:

> I said "Omeros,"
>
> and *O* was the conch-shell's invocation, *mer* was
> both mother and sea in our Antillean patois,
> *os*, a grey bone, and the white surf as it crashes
>
> and spreads its sibilant collar on a lace shore.
> Omeros was the crunch of dry leaves, and the washes
> that echoed from a cave-mouth when the tide has ebbed.
>
> The name stayed in my mouth.[46]

The Greek word is "derived" from elements of the French Creole dialect spoken, not written, on the islands and from the natural sounds of the Caribbean environment.[47] We may find in the apparent chronological inversion by which Greek derives from French a parallel to the device of ending an epic with a formula normally used for beginnings, although in the sounds of the natural environment the Narrator finds a linguistic source that is indeed older than language itself. What is more important is to recognize in the "demotion" of Greek to a derivative status relative to the primacy of "our Antillean patois"—itself a tellingly ironic formulation in a poem written chiefly in English—a motif repeated in at least two other central conceits with much broader thematic significance.

The first of these, a conceit descended from the idea of *translatio imperii*, involves the unending succession whereby formerly enslaved and colonized peoples become oppressors in their own right. The motif first appears in an early poem, "Ruins of a Great House," of which Rei Terada writes, "Walcott places the British conquest of St. Lucia at the end of an originless chain of conquests including the Roman colonization of Britain."[48] *Omeros* neatly extends this motif, beginning with the ancient Athenian democracy—"its *demos* demonic and its *ocracy* crass"—that enslaved its fellow Greeks who inhabited the islands of the Aegean in what began as a defensive league against Persian invasion, but ended as the Athenian Empire. Then Roman enslaved Greek and appropriated Greek culture as a symbol of its empire, passing this iconography of power on to other enslaved peoples destined to gain empires of their own. The British Empire in turn established colonies throughout the New World and, with its fellow European powers, enslaved and exterminated the inhabitants of that world—virtually in the case of the North American Iroquois and Sioux, completely in the case of the Antillean Aruacs and Caribs—and thereby created a fresh need for slaves, supplied by Africa, whose descendants remain oppressed by a racism particularly pervasive in the contemporary United States. But not even the enslaved and the oppressed are free from complicity. A shocked Achille witnesses a slaving raid carried out on his ancestral village by another African tribe.[49] The warlike Caribs had been responsible for wiping out the peaceful Aruacs, while a regiment of freed North American slaves—the "Buffalo Soldiers" of the U.S. Ninth Cavalry—advanced the cause of White imperialism by carrying out the final defeat of the Sioux.[50] "All colonies inherit their empire's sin."[51]

For our purposes a second motif is perhaps even more important: the figure of lineage or paternity in *Omeros* and in epic narrative generally. Paternity is a far from simple matter in *Omeros*. Dennis Plunkett grieves because he will die without an heir, and, in an act that is half pedantry and half unrestrained imagination, he appoints himself the "father" of a young midshipman, also named Plunkett, who died serving under Admiral Rodney in the Battle of Les Saintes 200 years before the story of *Omeros* takes place. Imagining this young man as his son does not prevent Plunkett from claiming him as an ancestor as well, by a crazy logic based on the fact that the young midshipman also died without leaving an heir. The Narrator stands in similarly ambiguous relation to his father, who died younger than his own present age; he thus figures himself as "older" than his father as he tells the story of *Omeros*.[52] During Achille's hallucinatory trip to Africa, he converses with people whom he imagines to be his ancestors; and, as the poem ends, he prepares to raise Helen's child, who may be his own son or that of his departed friend and rival, Hector. In all these instances, the father/son relationship is deeply problematized and its basis questioned: Is it primarily a biological relationship or one dependent on empathy, imaginative sympathy, mutual interest and acceptance, or even on an act of asserting will over reason? Does the vector of the relationship always follow the arrow of time from father to son, or does the son engender the father from whom he wishes to inherit?

This is one of the central problems of the European epic from its inception. The heroes of the *Iliad* are obsessed with their own ancestry and are bent on proving that they measure up to the standards set by their forebears. Telemachus's coming-of-age involves meeting his long-lost father for the first time in his life. Aeneas must transform himself from the dutiful son of a doomed race to the progenitor of the greatest empire in world history. Satan rebels against the appointed succession of the Father by the Son, so Adam, fatherless himself, becomes the begetter of humankind. It is difficult not to see in the career of the European epic an ideal instantiation of the Oedipal warfare that for Harold Bloom constitutes the driving force behind all literature. But the epigonal work can never overcome its own belatedness and derivative status. For epics such as these, genealogy—not just that of the hero, but that of the poem itself—becomes all important: by claiming legitimate descent from Homer, these epics attempt to take the place of Homeric epic as originary texts in their own right. On the grounds of originality, however, the principal European epics are compromised by their membership in a clearly defined literary tradition stretching back to Homer; hence they can never be original, as Homer is.

By renewing this aspect of the epic tradition, *Omeros* makes of itself a paradigm for the contemporary individual's relationship to the various cultural legacies that he or she inherits or wishes to claim. In a limited way, the poem can thus be read as an allegory of our own relationship to classical culture, or to the immigrant culture of our personal ancestors or even of groups to which we feel or imagine a sympathetic connection rather than an ethnic or biological one. The central reflection of this arrangement is the relative lack of authority and control that Walcott's Narrator exerts over his story, in sharp contrast to the objectivity and truth conventionally ascribed to the epic poet. The Narrator is thus not so far removed from his reader, in that both are in the position of needing to piece together fragments of a broken past in order to make sense of their existence and experiences.

Thus *Omeros* presents the reader with a litmus test, or rather with the illusion of such a test; for, like the bureaucrat of the story with which I began, any reader who seeks to apply such a test to this poem can only fail. There is in *Omeros* no black or white, but only black *and* white. Its roots are not in Europe *or* Africa, but necessarily in both. Consequently, *Omeros* cannot be epic *or* novel; it can only be epic *and* novel, however, if its relationship to classical epic—in whatever ways we problematize it—as well as to the epics of groups traditionally ignored by the canonical European tradition is fully acknowledged and integrated into our reading. This is only one of the reasons for celebrating this remarkable poem (which is, after all, still new to us, still in many ways uncanny and unfamiliar), for its ability to make us see our own past anew, to force us to reflect upon our own ancestry, and to understand our own heritage—racial, intellectual, and cultural—both as it is and as we would have it be.

## Notes

A version of this paper was presented at a conference on "Epics in the Contemporary World" at the University of Wisconsin on 22 April 1994. That version will appear in a volume based on the conference proceedings. I wish to thank Jane Tylus, Margaret Beissinger, and Susanne Lindgren Wofford, the principal conference organizers and editors of that volume, and the University of California Press for allowing this version of my paper to appear in *SAQ*.

1   For a brief bibliography and survey of the critical tradition, see Daniel Marowski and Roger Matuz, "Derek Walcott," *Contemporary Literary Criticism* 42 (1987): 414–23.

2   Derek Walcott, "A Far Cry from Africa," in *Collected Poems 1948–1984* (New York, 1994 [1986]), 18. The poem originally appeared in 1956 (according to Irma E. Goldstraw's indispensable *Derek Walcott: An Annotated Bibliography of His Works* [New York and London, 1984], 5) and was reprinted in Derek Walcott, *In A Green Night: Poems 1948–1960* (London, 1962), 18.

3   Derek Walcott, "The Hotel Normandie Pool," in *Collected Poems*, 443. The poem origi-

nally appeared in the *New Yorker* in 1981 (Goldstraw, *Derek Walcott*, 39) and, later that year, in Derek Walcott, *The Fortunate Traveller* (New York, 1981), 63–70.

4   See Mary Lefkowitz, "Bringing Him Back Alive," *New York Times Book Review*, 7 October 1990, 1, 34–35; B. M. W. Knox, "Achilles in the Caribbean," *New York Review of Books*, 7 March 1991, 3–4; Oliver Taplin, "Derek Walcott's *Omeros* and Derek Walcott's Homer," *Arion* 1 (1991): 213–26; and George Steiner, "From Caxton to *Omeros*," *Times Literary Supplement*, 27 August 1993, 13–16.

5   Sidney Burris, "An Empire of Poetry," *Southern Review* 27 (1991): 558–74; quotations from 559; my emphasis.

6   See Robert D. Hamner, *Derek Walcott*, rev. ed. (New York, 1993 [1981]), 19; cf. his introductory remarks in *Critical Perspectives on Derek Walcott*, ed. Robert D. Hamner (Washington, 1993), 10–12.

7   John Figueroa, "*Omeros*," in *The Art of Derek Walcott*, ed. Stuart Brown (Chester Springs, PA, 1991), 211.

8   Patricia Ismond, "Walcott's *Omeros*—A Complex, Ambitious Work," *Caribbean Contact* 18 (1991): 10–11.

9   Quoted by D. J. R. Bruckner, "A Poem in Homage to an Unwanted Man," *New York Times*, 9 October 1990, 13; rpt. in Hamner, ed., *Critical Perspectives*, 396. Walcott's remarks here also stress the importance to him of the novels of Rudyard Kipling, Joseph Conrad, and Ernest Hemingway as models for *Omeros*. See also Robert Brown and Cheryl Johnson, "Thinking Poetry: An Interview with Derek Walcott," *Cream City Review* 14 (1990): 209–33; and J. P. White, "An Interview with Derek Walcott," *Green Mountains Review*, new ser., 4 (1990): 14–37.

10   "*Omeros* is profoundly Homeric and undoubtedly epic" (Taplin, "Walcott's *Omeros* and Walcott's Homer," 213).

11   Burris, "Empire of Poetry," 560.

12   On dramatic elements in *Omeros*, see ibid., 561–64. Burris calls *Ulysses* "the work that will in all likelihood emerge as the most generous sponsor of *Omeros*" (561).

13   Figueroa, "*Omeros*," 203–5. He observes that St. Lucy, the patron saint of the island, was herself a blind seer (205). Blindness and compensatory insight is a recurring theme in Walcott's work, one with special relevance to the figure of the poet. In "Cul de Sac Valley," for example, Walcott images himself as an Oedipus questioned by a row of Sphinxes; see Derek Walcott, *The Arkansas Testament* (New York, 1987), 9–15; cf. Derek Walcott, *Epitaph for the Young* (Barbados, 1949), 10.

I capitalize "Narrator" here to distinguish the character in *Omeros* who narrates the poem and represents the figure of the poet himself from the "narrator," or implied singer, of whatever poem happens to be under discussion.

14   Figueroa, "*Omeros*," 206.

15   Brad Leithauser, "Ancestral Rhyme" (review of *Omeros*), *New Yorker*, 11 February 1991, 91–95. Cf. Figueroa, who observes, "The poem [is] much more a novel than an epic, while never losing its lyrical fire" ("*Omeros*," 197).

16   Bakhtin's argument is spelled out most clearly in his 1941 essay "Epic and Novel," in *The Dialogic Imagination: Four Essays*, ed. Michael Holquist, trans. Caryl Emerson and Michael Holquist (Austin, 1981), 3–40.

17   The question of Walcott's influences, which has been prominent in criticism of his work since the beginning, came to be viewed in terms of cultural allegiance as Walcott's European influences were found to be less relevant to the Africanist West Indian political consciousness of the 1960s and 1970s than the work of other writers, particularly Edward Brathwaite. The literature comparing these two writers is quite large: representative works include Edward Lucie-Smith, "West Indian Writing," *London Magazine* 8 (1968): 96–102; Arthur D. Drayton, "The European Factor in West Indian Literature," *Literary Half-Yearly* (Mysore) 11 (1970): 71–95; Louis James, "Caribbean Poetry in English—Some Problems," *Savacou* 2 (1970): 78–86; Anon., "How Far Are Derek Walcott and Edward Brathwaite Similar? Is It Impossible for the Caribbean to Choose between the Two, if So, Which Way Should They Choose and Why?" *Busara* 6 (1974): 90–100; Gordon Collier, "Artistic Autonomy and Cultural Allegiance: Aspects of the Walcott–Brathwaite Debate Reexamined," *Literary Half-Yearly* 20 (1979): 93–105; and Bruce King, "West Indies II: Walcott, Brathwaite, and Authenticity" (chap. 7), in *The New English Literatures: Cultural Nationalism in a Changing World* (New York, 1980), 118–39. As Walcott's interest in African themes, particularly evident in his plays *O Babylon!* and *Dream on Monkey Mountain*, came to be appreciated, the question of his cultural allegiances became less urgent. Further, with Walcott's rise to international stature came comparison with such poets as Joseph Brodsky and Seamus Heaney, and one result of appearing in such company on an international stage is that his Caribbean identity now seems hardly in doubt. Significantly, the West Indian writer to whom he is most often contrasted nowadays is not Brathwaite but V. S. Naipaul, with whose dismal judgment upon postcolonial culture, particularly in the West Indies, Walcott took exception in "The Caribbean: Culture or Mimicry?" *Journal of InterAmerican Studies and World Affairs* 16 (1974): 3–13; rpt. in Hamner, ed., *Critical Perspectives*, 51–57.

18   C. M. Bowra, *Heroic Poetry* (London, 1952), 1–11.

19   See Ruth Finnegan, *Oral Literature in Africa* (Oxford, 1970), 108ff. Finnegan is not concerned, however, as Bowra was, with the capacity of Africans to produce heroic literature so much as with the technical question of whether their heroic literature is in verse.

20   Of crucial importance was the publication of the Sundiata epic: D. T. Niane, *Sundjata, ou l'Epopée Mandingue* (Paris, 1960); *Sundiata: An Epic of Old Mali*, trans. G. D. Pickett (Harlow, 1965). On this poem, see Christopher L. Miller, *Theories of Africans: Francophone Literature and Anthropology in Africa* (Chicago, 1990), 87–101. Other important scholarly investigations of African epic include Isidore Okpewho, *The Epic in Africa: Toward a Poetics of the Oral Performance* (New York, 1979); and *Epic Poetry in Swahili and Other African Languages* (Leiden, 1983); as well as John William Johnson, "Yes, Virginia, There Is an Epic in Africa," *Research in African Literatures* 11 (1980): 308–26.

21   See A. B. Lord, *The Singer of Tales* (Cambridge, MA, 1960).

22   *Kambili*, Vol. 1 of *The Songs of Seydou Camara*, trans. Charles S. Bird, Mamadou Koita, and Bourama Soumaoro, ll. 505–7; quoted in Okpewho, *Epic in Africa*, 205–6.

23   A more apt comparison might have been between other instances of poet/audience interaction in contemporary performative epic and passages of our *Iliad* and *Odyssey* that are best explained as "local variants," or versions of the story suited to performance in some specific setting that somehow found their way into what eventually became

the "canonical" text. Such an explanation has been advanced for the episode involving Aeneas in *Iliad* 20, which may ultimately owe its existence to a ruling dynasty that claimed descent from the hero; see *The Iliad: A Commentary*, ed. G. S. Kirk; Vol. 5, ed. Mark Edwards (Cambridge, 1991), 298–301 (books 17–20), with further references. An even stronger case can be made for the prominence of the Athenian contingent in the "Catalogue of Ships" in that Athens was not a great power either when the events of the *Iliad* putatively occurred or when a recognizable version of the poem was first coming into existence; yet the Athenian tyrant Pisistratus played some role, one that may have been both extensive and decisive, in the canonization of the Homeric text that has come down to us. On this particular problem, see Kirk, ed., *Iliad*, Vol. 1 (Cambridge, 1985), 178–80 (books 1–4), with further references; on the phenomenon in general, see Jesper Svenbro, *La parole et le marbre: Aux origines de la poésie grecque* (Lund, 1976), 5–73.

24  This passage has a long history of interpretation, much of which finds the humorous element misplaced; see Kirk, ed., *Iliad*, Vol. 2 (Cambridge, 1990), 190–91 (books 5–8), with further references.

25  With this motif we may compare contemporary performances of North African epic; see Dwight Reynolds, "Complex Performances: Genres and Levels of Performance in the Event," in *Epics and the Contemporary World*, ed. Margaret Beissinger, Jane Tylus, and Susanne Lindgren Wofford (Berkeley: University of California Press, forthcoming).

26  Walcott, "Cul de Sac Valley," in *Arkansas Testament*, 9.

27  Ibid., 10.

28  Derek Walcott, *The Joker of Seville and O Babylon!* (New York, 1978), 155–56. This passage is quoted at greater length and discussed by Rei Terada, *Derek Walcott's Poetry: American Mimicry* (Boston, 1992), 93–94.

29  Derek Walcott, *Omeros* (New York, 1993 [1990]), 17–18 (1.3.2). Seven Seas performs, for instance, at a party held at the café in honor of a political candidate (2.20.1). Ma Kilman's eventual role as Philoctete's healer underlines the assonance between her name and that of Machaon, surgeon to the Greek forces in the *Iliad*, as Burris points out ("Empire of Poetry," 561), citing the equivalence as an example of Walcott's "slapstick disregard" for his Homeric parallels. Burris's rather facile reaction ignores the fact that the character of Ma Kilman, a "*gardeuse*, sybil, obeah-woman" (*Omeros*, 58 [1.10.2]), antedates the poem and indeed is first presented not as Walcott's creation but as a "found object" of St. Lucian folk culture, appearing first in a Creole song (both original and English translation) in "Sainte Lucie" (Walcott, *Collected Poems*, 314–19; first published in *Sea Grapes* as long ago as 1976). The connection with Machaon would appear to have been forged or "discovered" some time after the poet's initial acquaintance with the figure. I would add that the hand of the poet is more clearly visible in the character's connection with the No Pain Café, which takes its name from that of νηπενθής (*nepenthes*, "[allowing] no pain"), a drug administered by Helen to Menelaus and to their guests, Telemachus and Pisistratus, so that they might discuss the war at Troy and the difficult homecomings of the Greeks who fought there without succumbing to grief. Thus Ma Kilman herself is a type of Helen in her Odyssean, as opposed to her Iliadic, manifestation.

30  Walcott, *Omeros*, 154 (2.29.2).

31  Ibid., 283 (7.56.3).

32 The theme of alleged gaps in the author's reading recurs, again with respect to the sources of *Omeros* but this time involving the *Aeneid* as well as the *Odyssey*, in White, "Interview with Derek Walcott," 16–35. The problem is addressed with great insight by Mary Fuller, "Forgetting the *Aeneid*," *American Literary History* 4 (1992): 517–38. One thinks of Yeats's striking way of naming the inspiration of his life's work "the half-read wisdom of daemonic images" in "Meditations in Time of Civil War"; see *W. B. Yeats: The Poems, A New Edition*, ed. Richard J. Finneran (New York, 1983), 206.

33 Walcott, *Omeros*, 283 (7.56.3).

34 The theme of a natural language heard or even read in landscape is prominent throughout Walcott's work, as Terada indicates so well in *Derek Walcott's Poetry*, 152, 164–65, 167, and 171–74.

35 The locus classicus for this line of discourse is Friedrich Schiller's *Über naive und sentimentalische Dichtung* (1795–96). It continues in G. W. F. Hegel's *Ästhetik* (1835); on which see Andrew Bowie, *Aesthetics and Subjectivity from Kant to Nietzsche* (Manchester, 1990), 140–42; in Georg Lukács, *Theory of the Novel*, trans. Anna Bostock (Cambridge, MA, 1971 [1920]); in Erich Auerbach, *Mimesis*, trans. Willard R. Trask (Princeton, 1953 [1946]); and in Bakhtin's "Epic and Novel," which was not widely known in this country before the Emerson and Holquist translation of 1981. It is fair to say that although the influence of these thinkers on the study of the novel and its relationship not only to the epic but to premodern literature in general has been decisive, it has also been in many ways far from constructive.

36 Walcott, *Omeros*, 286–87 (7.57.1).

37 Ibid., 286.

38 Ibid., 286, 287.

39 Ibid., 320–21 (7.64.1).

40 Figueroa, "*Omeros*," 211; cf. the following couplet: (Narrator) " 'The gods and the demi-gods aren't much use to us.' / 'Forget the gods,' Omeros growled, 'and read the rest' " (Walcott, *Omeros*, 283 [7.56.3]).

41 On ancient allegoresis of Homer, see Robert Lamberton, *Homer the Theologian: Neoplatonist Allegorical Reading and the Growth of the Epic Tradition* (Berkeley, 1986), with further references. On *Paradise Lost*, see Lucy Newlyn, *Paradise Lost and the Romantic Reader* (Oxford, 1993). For a convenient survey of twentieth-century trends in Vergilian criticism, see *Oxford Readings in Vergil's Aeneid*, ed. S. I. Harrison (Oxford, 1990), 1–20.

42 This particular type of intertextuality goes by the convenient name *oppositio in imitando*. There is a considerable literature on this phenomenon, most of it known, unfortunately, only to specialists. For a brief survey with references, see the introduction to Joseph Farrell, *Vergil's Georgics and the Traditions of Ancient Epic: The Art of Illusion in Literary History* (New York and Oxford, 1991), 3–25. As a convenient illustration of the effect produced by this type of writing, consider the Narrator's observation that Achille's "end, when it comes, will be a death by water / (which is not for this book)." What is being imitated is Tiresias's prophecy in the *Odyssey* (11.134–36) that the hero's death will occur far from the sea. The *imitatio e contrario* not only redefines the meaning of death at sea according to the values of a new poetic universe, but actively enlists the contribution of a whole range of previous imitators of the *Odyssey*, from Dante, whose Ulisse does

in fact contradict Homer by dying a watery death (*Inferno* 26.85–142), to Kazantzakis, whose importance to Walcott as a mediator of Homeric and meta-Homeric traditions awaits further exploration, and to Eliot, particularly of course in *The Waste Land.*

The phenomenon of *oppositio in imitando* parallels what Harold Bloom has famously figured as the belated poet's struggle for originality in the face of an oppressive weight of tradition, in *The Anxiety of Influence: A Theory of Poetry* (London/Oxford/New York, 1973) and subsequent studies, although the focus of the former is on the impersonal forces of generic development rather than the psychological trope of the Oedipus complex. A further parallel may be found in the work of those scholars who have attempted to define the role of the individual poet/singer working within a tradition of oral composition and performance: see, for example, Michael Nagler, *Spontaneity and Tradition: A Study in the Oral Art of Homer* (Berkeley and Los Angeles, 1974); and Norman Austin, *Archery at the Dark of the Moon: Poetic Problems in Homer's Odyssey* (Berkeley and Los Angeles, 1975).

43  On this aspect of the *Aeneid*, see Michael C. J. Putnam, *The Poetry of the Aeneid: Four Studies in Imaginative Unity and Design* (Ithaca, 1988 [1965]), 151–201. On Milton's Christian revision of pagan heroism, see Stanley Fish, *Surprised by Sin: The Reader in Paradise Lost* (London and New York, 1967).

44  See David Quint, *Epic and Empire: Politics and Generic Form from Virgil to Milton* (Princeton, 1993); and Susanne Lindgren Wofford, *The Choice of Achilles: The Ideology of Figure in the Epic* (Stanford, 1992). (See also my review in *Bryn Mawr Classical Review* 4 [1993]: 481–89.)

45  The poem thus privileges orality over literacy: the modern spelling is identical to the ancient, but the rough-breathing mark is vestigial since the initial h-sound has disappeared. (Walcott uses it only at 3.30.2.) Walcott's transliteration of Homer's (Greek) name into Roman characters as "Omeros" thus ironically represents more accurately than standard Modern Greek orthography both the absence of the h-sound and the fact that the first and second o-sounds (represented in Greek by omicron and omega, respectively) no longer differ in quantity, as they did in the ancient language, but actually sound identical. In fact, to say even this is too simple in view of the multiplicity of ancient conventions of spelling and pronunciation and the modern distinction between Katharevusa and demotic. But my main point is, I think, clear.

46  Walcott, *Omeros*, 14 (1.2.3).

47  Note that it is clearly an inhabited or personified environment: a conch shell sounds only when blown like a horn; leaves crunch under human footsteps or from other causes; and the mouth of the cave quickly becomes the Narrator's mouth.

48  Terada, *Derek Walcott's Poetry*, 60; Derek Walcott, "Ruins of a Great House" (1956), in *Green Night*, 19–20; rpt. in *Collected Poems*, 19–21.

49  Walcott, *Omeros*, 206 (5.41.1), 207–9 (5.41.2–3), 144–45 (3.27.1).

50  "Buffalo Soldiers" was the name given by the Southwest and Plains Indians to the troops who served between 1866 and 1891 as the Ninth and Tenth Regiments of the U.S. Cavalry, all of them African Americans. The troops evidently accepted the name as a badge of honor, and the Tenth incorporated a bison into its regimental emblem; William H. Leckie, *The Buffalo Soldiers: A Narrative of the Negro Cavalry in the West* (Norman, 1967), 25–26. The Ninth's involvement in the U.S. government's response to the Ghost Dance

movement among the Sioux in 1890–91 was the last significant campaign by the Buffalo Soldiers (ibid., 252–60). The narrative of this episode in *Omeros* occurs in what may be the most elliptical part of the poem. It begins when Achille, fresh from his hallucinatory voyage to Africa, remembers hearing the Bob Marley song "Buffalo Soldier" at a party the previous night and imagines himself as a member of that troop (Walcott, *Omeros*, 161–62 [3.31.1]). The tale is related sporadically in the thirteen chapters (ending with book 5) that flow through the Narrator's experiences living in Boston and, especially, traveling to the Great Plains (a trip explicitly likened to Achille's dream of Africa at 4.34.2), and through passages narrated from the perspective of Catherine Weldon, a Bostonian who lived with Sitting Bull at the time of the Ghost Dance. Achille himself, in the reverie induced by Marley's music, is imagistically associated with the destruction of the Sioux Nation as well as the Aruacs (3.31.1). Similarly, Achille's ancestor, the Afolabe who first acquired the name Achilles from Admiral Rodney himself, helped the British forces position a cannon for the defense of St. Lucia against a French assault (2.14.3) and thereby unwittingly allied himself with the British Empire—which would ultimately gain political control over the island—and against the nation whose stamp on the island's culture, particularly its language and religion, would persist for his descendants. *Omeros* does not document the converse phenomenon, the complicity of American Indians in the enslavement of Blacks; see Annie Heloise Abel, *The American Indian as Slaveholder and Secessionist* (Lincoln, 1992 [1915]). And, to complete this brief typological survey of racial oppression, see Larry Koger, *Black Slaveowners: Free Black Slave Masters in South Carolina, 1790–1860* (Jefferson, NC, 1985).

51  Walcott, *Omeros*, 208 (5.41.2).

52  "'Now that you are twice my age, which is the boy's / which the father's?' / 'Sir,'—I swallowed—'they are one voice'" (ibid., 68 [1.12.1]).

**Timothy Hofmeister**

# Classical Analogy as Discursive Act: A Reading of Derek Walcott's "As John to Patmos"

That Derek Walcott's most recent works, *Omeros* and *The Odyssey: A Stage Version*, involve the Western classical tradition[1] so extensively comes as less of a surprise when one considers that his serious engagement with the classical tradition began with his earliest work. Throughout a long career, Walcott's transactions with that tradition have been intense, expressive, full of contradictions—in short, a rich and integral part of his work. *In A Green Night*, which was only Walcott's third collection of poetry, contains a number of poems dealing with classical subjects and motifs,[2] including "As John to Patmos," where we can see the relation to the classics already being worked out according to what would become a typical (i.e., complex) strategy.

Walcott frames the correspondence of the poem's narrative "I" to John of Patmos in terms of a formal analogy. Strictly speaking, of course, analogy represents one thing by comparing it with some other thing that shares certain features, but not every feature, with the original object of representation. I will sometimes use the term less restrictedly, however, when speaking of other Walcott poems, to denote their respec-

The *South Atlantic Quarterly* 96:2, Spring 1997.
Copyright © 1997 by Duke University Press.

tive constructed relations of modern to ancient artifact. Some poems that deal with the Greek and Roman classics cast the relation in the precise form of an analogical simile, but just as often a classical motif is attached as metaphor or a specific ancient text is engaged, wholly or partly, in an extended intertextual allusion. In all instances, it becomes necessary to read the modern poem with the ancient motif or text constantly in mind. It is the totality of these recontextualizations and allusions, whatever the technical means that bring them about, which constitutes Walcott's relation to the tradition of classical antiquity.

In "As John to Patmos," Walcott constructs the analogy between John of the *Apokalypsis* (Revelation) and the poem's narrator, and also between Patmos, the exilic island of John, and Walcott's own island of St. Lucia or another island of the Lesser Antilles, on the basis of two points of resemblance. First, the Greek island's "blue, live air" is equated to the "blue scapes" of the Caribbean. Second, the fact of exile itself links John, who was exiled on Patmos probably in the reign of Domitian, to the narrator, who vows to "voyage no more from home."[3] The latter produces an asymmetry, however, since Patmos was not "home" to John in the same way as the Caribbean island is to the narrator. And yet it will soon be clear that the management of this analogy is a complicated process—for the poet and so, necessarily, for the reader. Once it is apparent, for instance, how the island both is and is not home to the narrator, then its relation to Patmos is at once revived. Indeed, throughout the poem, the poet no sooner introduces similarities between the Aegean and Antillean islands than he breaks them down, nor interrupts the sense of identity for very long before offering some nuance to restore it.[4] This back-and-forth movement constitutes a manipulation of analogy by a progressive articulation of both the affinities and the disparities of its terms, or what I would identify as the discursive use of analogy.[5]

———

The first two stanzas of "As John to Patmos" formally institute the analogy of John's epiphany on Patmos and the narrator's experience of his own island:

> As John to Patmos, among the rocks and the blue, live air, hounded
> His heart to peace, as here surrounded

> By the strewn-silver on waves, the wood's crude hair, the rounded
> Breasts of the milky bays, palms, flocks, the green and dead
>
> Leaves, the sun's brass coin on my cheek, where
> Canoes brace the sun's strength, as John, in that bleak air,
> So am I welcomed richer by these blue scapes, Greek there,
> So I shall voyage no more from home; may I speak here.[6]

The interlocking order of "John"/"there" and "here"/"I" might seem a ponderous device for initiating the analogy. But the highly articulated balancing, summed up by "Greek there" and "speak here," may also be taken as an opposition. The elaborate syntax actually distinguishes "there" and "here" as much as it unites them. The narrator's statement of affinity, or relation, to John and Patmos thus affirms a distance, and a difference, from them at one stroke.

The poet manages a similar effect in working out the likeness of the atmosphere and light of John's island to his own. This would seem at first to be a simple correspondence. John's setting on Patmos, described in the first line ("As John to Patmos, among the rocks and the blue, live air"), seems to promote an analogy to the Caribbean. But when that characterization is revised in the second stanza ("as John, in that bleak air"), similitude begins to dissolve.[7] The result is indeed not resemblance but a widening contrast when St. Lucia is described in detail: bright ("strewn-silver"), wild ("the wood's crude hair"), and sensual ("the rounded / Breasts of the milky bays"). The poet not only stresses the stunning physical impact that the island makes upon the observer, but also hints at the intrinsic strength of its people ("where / Canoes brace the sun's strength"). The accounts of the two islands become increasingly disproportionate; in the most obvious terms, the poet's island simply gets more attention. Then its superiority to John's place is at last made explicit near the end of the second stanza ("So am I welcomed richer by these blue scapes").

Not that the poet's island is rendered without any irony: "the wood's crude hair" rings favorably in a Romantic sense of unspoilt Nature, but "crude" also connotes "unkempt," "uncultivated." The suggestion of a lack of cultivation invokes in turn the question of culture, namely, whether the Caribbean has anything of the sort, a frustrating burden Walcott often assumes in his poems (e.g., "the merciless idiocy of green, green"[8]). Moreover, the sensuality of the "milky bays" is appealing on one level, yet on another level is troubling, such as in these two lines from a poem that follows shortly after "As John to Patmos": "Teach our philosophy the strength to reach / Above the navel."[9] True, it is hard to say if this is an earnest prayer: the sight of "black bodies" rolling in surf at the end of that poem is embarrassingly wanton, ostensibly, but it also positively portends a restless vitality.

Perhaps most disturbing is the imagery of coins deployed so prominently in the first two stanzas of "As John to Patmos." It is not unusual for Walcott to brush in the shimmering surface of water by means of such handy images as coins, metals, fish scales—all of which appear frequently in such descriptions. On the other hand, this poem is based on a wholly explicit and extended reference to the New Testament. Read in that light, the coin images take on a negative cast: "strewn-silver" would evoke Judas's thirty pieces, the reward for his betrayal, and "brass coin" would echo the "sounding brass" of Paul's famous letter to the Corinthians. Even as the poet steers one's reception of the Greece/Antilles analogy in favor of the latter, in other words, one is pulled, as if in a counter-eddy, out of a secure satisfaction with "home." What impels this current is self-condemnation. If it is the poet's cheek on which the sun's "brass coin" rests, then, by extension, it is he who collects the Judas-silver. He becomes not merely a hollow vessel but the faithless follower as well.

Such a shift would seem to alienate the poet from his native island. That sort of alienation might in turn begin to make sense of the analogous exiles. It is time, then, to turn to John's exile, which the poet characterizes in an unexpected way: "As John to Patmos, among the rocks and the blue, live air, hounded / His heart to peace." What is striking is that, by this account, John's sojourn on lonely Patmos had nothing to do with a political sentence imposed during the persecutions of the Church under Domitian. The poet recasts that exile as a personal affair, and so the "hounding" John suffered was self-imposed. But to what exactly does this "hounding" refer? Having the text of Revelation in mind, one might be inclined to say that the poet means John "hounded his heart" out of anger at a world he saw deteriorating around him. The "peace" his heart finally achieved would, on this reading, refer to a catharsis, which John experienced after responding to the world's wickedness through the violence of the *Apokalypsis*.

Yet it is difficult to see how any analogy between John and the narrator could help explain in what way the latter has "hounded" his own "heart." Writing with none of the anger or violence that fills Revelation, the poet attributes a "peace" to John that must relate to the elation with which he envisioned a new world arising after the destruction of the old. The first sentence of the third stanza does indeed advert to precisely that Johannine motif of the birth of a new heaven and a new earth: "This island is heaven." So the "peace" of John parallels and thus illuminates a peace the narrator has won. Formally, however, the analogy juxtaposes John's hounding his heart with the action—or nonaction—promised by the narrator's declaration: "So I shall voyage no more from home." It follows, then, that the sense in which he has "hounded" his own "heart" must also depend, perversely, on the beauty and paradisal quality of the island. This is a paradox which the relation to John now seems to necessitate: on one hand, a basic similarity is implied, namely, the apparent conviction that the island is a heaven like John's; on the other hand, the poet's special inflection of John's experience suggests that this very "heaven" is what hounds his heart. Certain key contrasts between John's vision and the poet's are meant to highlight the disturbing side of the paradox—contrasts that will be foregrounded once we begin to cut against the grain of this reading.

Before we press the paradox in that direction, however, we need to explore further the congruities of John's apocalyptic account to the poet's revelation of his island's otherworldly beauty. A shared bias underlies both the poet's praise of his new heaven and the prophet's wrath against the old earth: an antipathy toward the city. John's survey of the seven churches early in his work reveals his low opinion of the great cities of Asia Minor. These churches are either warned to purge themselves of evils (such as the teaching of the Nicolaitans) or, if praised, are urged all the same to shun the doom that impends for the wicked. The city of Sardis in particular is simply told to repent its evil. When one comes right down to it, the allegory of the Whore of Babylon hardly leaves much doubt about John's view of his contemporary urban civilization.

So in "As John to Patmos," Walcott formulates the island's "heavenly" quality in contrast to the deterioration of the city: "This island is heaven— away from the dustblown blood of cities." Clearly showing the influence of Eliot, not to mention St. John Perse (especially the Perse of *Anabase*), the indictment of desiccated cities here also looks forward to a passage like the following:

> From here he could see the dreck
> under the scrolled skirts of statues, the grit in the stone lions'
> eyes; he saw under everything an underlying grime
>
> that itched in the balls of rearing bronze stallions.[10]

This city is London — Eliot's, it could be, with the added dross of a generation or two. In his pointed description of London's physical decadence, the narrator speaks for the wandering poet Seven Seas, or Omeros, who is taking in the signs of the creeping ruin of the imperial capital. As a whole, this portion of *Omeros* represents the narrator's (counter-)exploration of the Old World, beginning with Portugal, appropriately enough, whose capital, Lisbon, symbolizes all the ports whence the ships, soldiers, and slavers of the great empire-building nations embarked. Rather than locating, in this reverse voyage of discovery, the center of worldly dominion, however, the narrator finds that those older powers are worn-out and rotting, or crumbling, away.

In "As John to Patmos," there is a hint, but perhaps only a hint, of that sort of critique, which examines the Old World, and its great cities, as the source of slavery and imperialism. When Walcott alludes to such cities as withered, hence unproductive, what this plainly implies is that the Old World has lost its vitality, and so is failing to reproduce itself. At the same time, the New World has been born, and is waiting to be born. Together, the depictions of island and metropolitan worlds make a political gesture, though a subtle one. Otherwise the poem does not engage in overt political argument and displays none of the violence and aggression of John's text — think of the horrid feast of the birds at the climax of the battle against the Beast (Rev. 19:17–21).

Walcott seems more concerned with how "the dustblown blood of cities" points up, by contrast, what makes the island — the new heaven-on-earth — lovely:

> This island is heaven — away from the dustblown blood of cities;
> See the curve of bay, watch the straggling flower, pretty is
> The wing'd sound of trees, the sparse-powdered sky, when lit is
> The night. For beauty has surrounded
> Its black children, and freed them of homeless ditties.[11]

Clearly, this stanza, like the first one, aims to represent the natural beauty of the island, although the phrases "straggling flower" and "sparse-powdered sky" seem to be qualified in an odd way, almost pejoratively. But it is more likely that these are descriptive turns which Walcott has tuned carefully to suggest a nascent landscape, the incipient state of which corresponds to the poetic representation of its beauty. The last two lines of the stanza echo John's description of the moment when God will return to his people, his vision of the New Jerusalem:

> He will dwell among them and they shall be his people, and God himself will be with them. He will wipe every tear from their eyes. There shall be an end to death, and to mourning and crying and pain, for the old order has passed away. (Rev. 21:3–4)

John's New Jerusalem is a city of light (Rev. 21:23–24), which Walcott translates as "when lit is / The night." The clause is crucial to the structure of the third stanza—its acme, in fact, where the images of its first two lines converge—and its bridge, linking the first half of the stanza to the conclusion. In conception, "when lit is / The night" also parallels John's claim, toward the end of his account, that the new city needs neither sun nor moon, since the glory of God illuminates it (Rev. 21:23), as well as echoing this pair of verses from the end of *Another Life*: "Gregorias, listen, lit, / we were the light of the world!" [12] What both Walcott passages express has to do, first of all, with the pun on "lit," which can mean "illuminated" or "drunk," so both sets of lines add a sense of intoxication, or arousal, to the image of light. The excitement in "As John to Patmos" at the discovery of a radiantly beautiful place arises not from John's conviction that the beauty has a divine source but from the narrator's newly awakened wonder at that beauty itself. The exclamation at the conclusion of *Another Life*, however, stems from a new faith in the power of art to exalt human existence, although this exuberance is also evocative of the power of friendship.

So long as one reads "As John to Patmos" along these lines, developing the faithful—though highly selective—analogy to the text of John, what one reads is a song of love and praise:

> As John to Patmos, in each love-leaping air,
> O slave, soldier, worker under red trees sleeping, hear
> What I swear now, as John did:
> To praise lovelong, the living and the brown dead. [13]

The narrator attributes to John the qualities of love ("As John . . . in each love-leaping air") and praise ("What I swear now, as John did: / To praise

lovelong"), yet his prophetic book hardly seems like a love-text, nor anyone's encomium, unless it is the Son's. John does, in fact, praise the elect
who gather around their God to sing *his* praises. In addition, John implicitly bestows love and praise on the faithful, who had not forsaken the
name of Christ—those of the so-called first resurrection (Rev. 20:4–6).
Likewise, those living such lives at the time, he seems to imply, will enter
the kingdom without delay: "Happy are those who wash their robes clean!"
(Rev. 22:14). Drawing this mindfulness of a faithful elect from John's narrative, Walcott sings the praise of his own people, who are saved from
slavery. (We will return to the remarkably oblique introduction of slavery,
i.e., as "homelessness.") Poet and people have found a new home in their
island and its natural beauty, and, since recognition of that home prom-
ises abundant new life, circumstances seem to require the poet to find his
own satisfaction in fostering that recognition.

───────

So much for the elating discourse of the poem. What I have called the
close, or "faithful," analogy to John's text effectively partitions him, that is,
it walls off the wrath of his account of the "last things." Walcott focuses instead on love, that love upon which the Christian community was based—
ideally, at least—in John's time. Although love figures in the latter's narrative, it is only at the end,[14] in his vision of the New Jerusalem, which is
actually the Christian community projected into a future that transcends
both the persecutions of and the feuds and derelictions within John's contemporary church.

The poet's approach to John is therefore, as we have indeed already
noted, a highly selective one. Walcott *works* the analogy to the prophet in
order to bring out of John's apocalyptic song one of love and praise. In
the process, however, the particular circumstances surrounding the poet's
song shape its composition, even as he is carrying on his dialogue with the
ancient writer. After all, the wrath of John, which the poet rehabilitates in
order to translate the prophet within a modern lyric, reflects John's own
response to the historical context in which he himself composed. So, too,
is this early poem of Walcott's complicated by the need to address a specific historical situation.

Turning now to some of the troubling aspects of the poem, the third
stanza in particular represents the poet's coming to grips with history,

social change, and the evolution of his own culture. One's attention is drawn to these difficulties all the more forcefully by the way in which parts of John's text have been rewritten or abandoned, while its relation to the poem has been ineradicably impressed on the reader's consciousness for the duration of the lyric. Indeed, Walcott anticipates that consciousness in the turns of his poem, such as by making beauty (rather than God) what returns to (or "surrounds") the lost people—an alteration of John's vision that exposes a gulf between God and the former slaves of the island. While the expectation of a closer relationship to God derives from the reader's knowledge of John's narrative, the poet's inflection of that narrative blocks any such consolation.

It is expressive of the same comfortlessness that beauty—whose children the island's are said to be—is genderless: "its." Denied God the Father, one might have hoped for their adoption by Mother Beauty as compensation. Yet beauty seems to lack gender in order to withhold such comfort. Furthermore, the narrator contextualizes, or historicizes, that sense of separation and disconsolateness when he refers to the era of slavery by juxtaposing "black children" with "freed them of homeless ditties." Under this historicizing influence, we would want to read "when lit is / The night" differently. Opposed to what the phrase would mean in John's context—that night has become as day—the context here suggests that day has become as night. Historicized, finally, this reversal of night and day would symbolize a new stage in history, one in which it could confidently be said that a previously displaced Black culture had taken root, for example, among the islands of the Caribbean.

The way we are now reading the poem makes clearer at what price (or in what coin) the poet's island has paid for its beauty. We also begin to understand at last—a crucial step in reading the lyric—why the narrator has had to "hound" himself to "peace": the memory of slavery is a burden that must be thrown off before he can feel "welcomed richer" by a landscape that will otherwise reveal to him only the recent history of oppression. This is just one way, however, in which John's "hound[ing] / His heart" may be relevant to the narrator's own experience, for the latter is also "hounded" by the fear that the transplanted culture of his new region is stillborn or stifled. This is a crucial concern, as is demonstrated by the rhymes of the third stanza. If these rhymes seem forced—"cities" / "pretty is" / "lit is" / "ditties"—the poet may have intended them to be. It is conceivable that they are performative, that their jingling sound actually *enacts* what the narrator laments at the end of the stanza: "homeless ditties."[15] The poet himself has composed—that is, played at composing or composed mimetically—a "ditty," or "love-leaping air": a trivial or self-indulgent song. In this interpretation, the tone becomes a truth-telling one, a confession of anxiety that perhaps beauty's children are not yet "freed . . . of homeless ditties." Thus we return to the issue raised earlier: the poet's sense of alienation from his own people. Having already hinted at his sense of being some sort of betrayer of his cause, the narrator's ironic expression here of his own qualms about "lack of culture," a stigma occasioned by the complex history of his region, reveals a root of his lack of faith.

Walcott may, on the other hand, be expressing the impulse of an emerging culture to be liberated from what is perceived as an inferior stage of development, that is, to be free of the perception itself, which is both invidious and false. Those same "bad rhymes" make the point. Their impact is moderated by means of enjambment, which is deliberately employed in the first and third stanzas but not in the second or fourth. The first and third stanzas are given over to descriptions of the island, and it might be said, rather crudely, that this is a congenial subject. Or, better, the island as pristine setting for the new culture—a fresh creation in which all things wait for their proper names—is what the poet's song is supposed to be about, so in those parts of the poem where the island appears in its proper aspect, this song flows most freely, as the enjambed lines render vividly, almost performatively.

The second and fourth stanzas are unenjambed, and here the voice is John's, or rather a facsimile of it. One need only note the mood of the verbs throughout the poem to recognize the kind of speech effect for which the poet is striving. The second stanza ends with a declarative future, "So I shall," and an optative, "may I speak here." The moods of the verbs in the third and fourth stanzas make an even more marked impression, as a high percentage of them are imperatives: "see," "watch," "hear." This use of commands reveals the poet's wish to abandon "ditties" for a kind of poetic speech that is powerful, revelatory, even epoch-making—thus the vehemence of "hear / What I swear now." Plainly, the forceful rhetoric derives from a will to replicate John's powerful testification. The management of enjambment lets the poet modulate—behind the poem, so to speak—from a gentle, ironizing voice to an urgent, would-be authoritative—"prophetic"—one, and back again.

In striving for this prophetic tone, the aim is to elevate this song to a level of public, hence historical, significance—an end also served by the allusion to the cruelty of the past in the last stanza: "O slave, soldier, worker under red trees sleeping." If the memory of slavery cannot be expunged, then, as in cases of trauma, at least new growth may slowly displace the injured portions of body or psyche. So, in this concluding stanza, the poet appears to find a means of easing his own lack of comfort with either the recent history or the present prospects of the local culture. Beside the slave lie the soldier and the worker, each representing a new stage of history that has constituted itself after the actual experience of slavery is over. On the face of it, then, this line constructs an image of progress by the poet's people and, given what we have seen of the poet's sensitivity over cultural accomplishment, one in which he may finally be able to share.

But here again, the poet's ironic spirit intrudes, and the workings of irony undercut this idea of progress. Soldiers and workers are themselves always subject to some power or another. One must wonder about these dead.[16] Perhaps the soldier served in a foreign campaign and returned alive but maimed, like the "veteran of the African campaign" in "Two Poems on the Passing of an Empire," whose "balsam eye" and "empty sleeve" reveal his sacrifice, and who passes the remainder of his life "in the small coffin of his house" (i.e., in a kind of death-in-life).[17] The juxtaposition of worker and "red trees" in "As John to Patmos," however, raises the suspicion that suffering, even violence, attends this figure, too. Perhaps what we have here is a terse allusion to labor unrest and its bloody outcome— the "red trees" suggesting both social activism and bloodshed—such as appears later in "Roseau Valley."[18] Here, in any case, the poet's difficulty with coming to rest in his, and his people's, "home" remains.

The last line of the poem, which seems at first a resounding affirmation of the poet's resolve, and of a connection with his people, poses the same sort of difficulty: "To praise lovelong, the living and the brown dead." The problem lies in the line's ambiguity. On one hand, "the living" and "the brown dead" can be construed as two different groups, which would effect an alarming disjunction. If the living, who now settle into "this island . . . heaven," have to forget the brown dead, for whom the island was no heaven at all, then the poem points us toward a deracinated future. We must then ask if this repression of memory will in turn threaten the poet with future spiritual upheaval.[19] On the other hand, "the living and the brown dead" may designate a single group, the dead, who are both living and brown.

This option recovers the tone of praise, since the dead are not separated from the living in that negative way we just considered, but are exalted. They are *brown* (and we know now what that cost), yet they are also *living*, which would recall John's triumphalism in its most generous aspect: his fervent assertion of the reality of the resurrection.

The ambiguity here resists reduction to just one of these readings. It would be misguided to resolve the tension between a harmonious vision of the communion of the dead and living and the despairing contemplation of their divorce. It is worth noting in this connection that the poem following "As John to Patmos" in this volume is "Elegy," dedicated to Walcott's father. The father seems vividly present in that poem, such as in the reckoning that this is his "seventeenth death," a provocative rendering that turns the tables on conventional assumptions about life and death, and in that sense restores the absent father. But by the end of the poem, it is uncertain what advantage one can gain over death:

> For greater than death is death's gift, that can,
> Behind the bright dust that was the skeleton,
>
> (Who drank the wine and believed the blessed bread)
> Can make us see the forgotten price of man
> Shine from the perverse beauty of the dead.[20]

"Death's gift" is ultimately a gain only for the living. If that gift teaches us patience in facing the loss occasioned by death, it hardly seems to close the gulf between the dead, who have gone, and the living, who must remain. The modification of eucharistic language—"believed the blessed bread"—dismisses the blessing of the loaf, the mystical, transformative act itself, and replaces it with "believed," putting a great deal of pressure on that operation (which in this theological context would seemingly be necessary but not sufficient to defeat death). "Elegy" ends as ambiguously as "Patmos" does: Is the "price," if forgotten, nevertheless redeemed? Or is it irredeemable? And, of course, the handsome phrase "the perverse beauty of the dead" gives absolutely nothing of its uncertainty away.

The diffident position taken vis-à-vis the dead in "Elegy" and in "As John to Patmos" constitutes one more contrast with John's text. In this respect, John has an enormous advantage, since his account is based on the premise that Christ has defeated death. As ready to hand as this postulate might seem, however, we should not underestimate the profoundly dramatic quality with which John invests the idea. After pronouncing Jesus Christ ὁ πρωτότοκος τῶν νεκρῶν ("the first-born of the dead") upon his first sight of the Christ figure, John falls down at his feet "like a dead man" (Rev. 1:5, 17). This figure lays his right hand upon John and says, to comfort him, that he—Jesus—is living, though he was dead. Death fundamentally underlies John's text and goads the fierce desire of its eschatology, yet so does a reasonably vital doctrine that renders the denouement of his poetic drama of Death's defeat plausible.

While a detailed discussion of Walcott's relationship to traditional Christian belief is beyond the scope of this essay, what can be said is that Walcott, true to the complexity of his times and his own ironic tendencies, lacks that very doctrinal foundation. (Not that we do not also pay a terrific price for John's eschatological exhilaration: as resounding as the triumph of his apocalypse is, so much the greater must our sense of the evil now with us be.) The poet of "As John to Patmos" likewise lacks the means to present the dilemma of reconciling life and death as in any way decidable. Here again, Walcott uses the distance between John's stance and his own on the vital issue of death and resurrection, and on the nature of our relation to the dead, to deepen our awareness of the ambiguity of praising "lovelong, the living and the brown dead"—and no doubt to underscore the fragility of his own "peace."

The kind of literary analogy we have traced in "As John to Patmos" turns out to be a complex and highly expressive poetic act. The relation with John that Walcott constructs and elaborates here is a means of articulating the conditions of his own time and place, including the conditions under which poetry is written. Contradictions arise in this relation because the bases of affinity are numerous but so too are the differences in historical context and ideological and spiritual orientation. There are contradictions that arise in Walcott's immediate milieu, after all, such as his being Methodist, middle class, and of mixed African and European descent, living on a poor, mostly Catholic, and only recently decolonized island. The tensions inherent in these polarities tend to energize Walcott's poetry, however, as has long been recognized, while the difficulties and dissonances created by his classical/mythological analogies have enriched his poems to the same extent.

Accordingly, the sort of discursive analogy that underpins "As John to Patmos" is all the more eloquent for exposing the differences that lie side by side with similarities. Analogy is a frequent mode in the other poems of *In A Green Night*. "Anadyomene," for example, depicts a girl diving into the sea by means of an extended comparison to a composite figure, a conflation of Aphrodite rising from the sea, after her birth in the foam, and another classical figure, the sea-nymph, or Nereid. Here the poet seems to want the archetypal depth of these ancient but foreign figures to incarnate an experience that strikes him as perhaps more than local, indeed more than merely human. Rarely is classical analogy utilized in Walcott's poetry in so naive a form.[21] One may compare "Anadyomene," however, with an apograph from the same page of Walcott's notebook, the poem "Choc Bay," also from *In A Green Night*. Again, a woman is diving into the sea, and the poem entails a decision whether to imagine her as Venus or as the Virgin. That Venus loses out ("Venus lives with aristocrats") should signal the rejection of classical analogy as a tool of perception or medium of poetic discourse. On the contrary, however, the poem forestalls that rejection in two ways. First, Venus is never truly dismissed:

> Not for the shell of the wailing dawn,
> For Venus dead in green water,
> Not for her, windmourned, wave murmuring over daughter,
> Who nets the mussels in goldwoven hair.[22]

Second, the poem ends in banishment, or "flight from paradise," just as in the Fall, with the fateful knowledge in this case (in one reading) amounting to a loss of innocent faith in the transcendence of the Mary of folk belief.

Walcott's later poem "Origins" also seems to dismantle the foundations of analogy to classical antiquity. "I learnt your annals of ocean, / Of Hector, bridler of horses, / Achilles, Aeneas, Ulysses." The poet studied these annals because his proper tradition was lost, and the imposition of an extrinsic culture preempted a true indigenous one. The poem gradually attempts to erase this colonial culture from its consciousness, just as its native culture was erased by history: "The mind, among sea-wrack, sees its mythopoeic coast, / Seeks, like the polyp, to take root in itself."[23] So the poet asks for a new song, which should preclude any dialogue with the classics. And yet, the figure on whom the poet focuses in the final section of "Origins" is none other than Odysseus:

> The sea waits for him, like Penelope's spindle,
> Ravelling, unravelling its foam,
> Whose eyes bring the rain from far countries, the salt rain
> That hazes horizons and races,
> Who, crouched by our beach fires, his face cracked by deserts,
> Remembering monarchs, asks us for water
> Fetched in the fragment of an earthen cruse,
> And extinguishes Troy in a hissing of ashes,
> In a rising of cloud.[24]

This Odysseus may seem humbled, like one who has passed through the absurdist or modernist fires of Beckett and Perse. But for all that, this conception of the hero is not so different from Homer's when he compares Odysseus to a spark kept alive in a bed of embers, or when Odysseus later supplicates Alcinous and Arete from the ashes of their hearth, or when, at the end of the *Odyssey*, in his bloody rags he awaits Penelope's word.

Walcott's frequent explorations of the device put it to the test, but analogy is never disavowed. Again, those poems that seem harshest or appear to disallow any significant relation between the modern Antillean poet and classical antiquity yield strenuous and highly productive negotiations within such relations. In the relatively recent "From This Far," for example, the discursive movement again asserts a break with the classical past:

> but no stone head rolls in the ocher dust,
> in the soil of our islands no gods are buried.
> They were shipped to us, Seferis,
> dead on arrival.[25]

The poet breaks with an ideology founded on the amalgamation of foreign and local (Caribbean) traditions. But the repudiative tone is immediately undermined by the choice of addressee: Seferis. By speaking throughout to a Greek poet, Walcott closes the very rift he opened. Reading this poem closely soon makes it clear that the whole composition is rich in Seferis's favorite themes: the haunting of the poet by long-dead friends, erotic memories that plague an aging poet, and the difficulty (and necessity) of lifting, by one's own meager strength, the heavy stone head of the past.

In "From This Far," Walcott implicitly honors Seferis's sense of craft by the very act of address, but he also pays tribute to Seferis's lifelong—

or "lovelong"—spiritual struggle, his attempt to translate and reinterpret a 3,000-year-old cultural heritage that he perceived as stretching toward him from Mycenae and Asine:

> Dawn buckles on the helmet
> of rayed Agamemnon.
> A net is flung over the shallows;
> ocean divides: a bronze door.
> In the wash the trunks of warriors
> roll and recede.
> Great lines, Seferis, have heaved them this far.[26]

In spite of their diverse circumstances, Walcott's desire to communicate with, as well as through, the spirit of the ancient tradition is as acute as Seferis's and his ingenuity in encompassing that desire is hardly matched by any other contemporary poet.

### Notes

This essay was written mainly while I was Blegen Research Fellow for 1995–96 in Classics at Vassar College. I would like to thank my colleagues there for the stimulating atmosphere they provided, as well as for their friendship. I was also fortunate to have the opportunity to present much of the material in this essay to a meeting of the NEH seminar "Homer's *Iliad* and Derek Walcott's *Omeros*," conducted by Professor William Shullenberger of Sarah Lawrence College (24 June–26 July 1996). I am grateful to Bill and his group for their kind invitation, and for a lively and highly productive session.

1  For an early discussion of Homer's presence in *Omeros*, see Timothy Hofmeister, "Iconoclasm, Elegy and Epiphany: Derek Walcott Contemplating the Bust of Homer," *International Journal of the Classical Tradition* 1 (1994): 107–28.

2  Derek Walcott, *In A Green Night: Poems 1948–1960* (London, 1962). These "classical" poems are "As John to Patmos," "Choc Bay," "Two Poems on the Passing of an Empire," "Greenwich Village, Winter," "Anadyomene," "A Sea-Chantey," "Roots," and "Bronze."

3  Walcott, "As John to Patmos," in *Green Night*, 12.

4  Analogy holds dangers, of course, such as the choice of comparison's limiting what one sees in an object. Also, comparison of two objects of different provenance may imply that one, especially if it is less known, is inferior, a problem cited at the end of "Allegre" (*Green Night*, 58–59), which represents a morning in the Caribbean by twice alluding to Italy:

> Yet to find the true self is still arduous,
> And for us, especially, the elation can be useless and empty
> As this pale, blue ewer of the sky,
> Loveliest in drought.

As the classical tradition has not been free of ideological shaping, analogy that draws on it is often politically suspect. Analogy is epistemologically suspect as well, as Rei Terada suggests in *Derek Walcott's Poetry: American Mimicry* (Boston, 1992): "Analogy is never absolute, but it is the imperfect vehicle of discernment" (196). And yet, because Walcott is constructing his own relation to the classics even as he creates each analogy, his analogies tend in fact to be critical and antihegemonic.

Take another example from "Allegre." The analogue in the first instance is Italy: "And the sunward side of the shacks / Gilded, as though this was Italy." In the second instance, the analogue becomes *young* Italy: "Laughter and doves, like young Italy." This shift is expressive and, in signifying that Italy is no longer young, insinuates that Italy now may lack beauty or freshness—qualities that have begun to manifest themselves in a new part of the world. "Allegre" thematizes the risks of analogy, then, but manages at the same time to critique the older, "superior" term from within the comparison, illustrating the critical or discursive capacity of analogy.

5 In describing his conduct of analogy as a "back-and-forth movement," I borrow from Walcott himself, that is, from one explanation he has given for writing poetry ("Caligula's Horse," in *After Europe: Critical Theory and Post-Colonial Writing*, ed. Stephen Slemon and Helen Tiffin [Sydney, 1989], 139):

> I have always thought in two margins. It has been the rigid benediction of my life, and to think in two margins—one on the right, and one on the left, obviously—is to serve a life-long sentence. To live out a pun. . . . So, you see what happens when poets are asked to think with only one margin, that of the left, unless they are Korean, or Hebrew, writing in the wrong direction, but still with the sense of that other approaching margin, that versus at the end of which the plough turns, those primary gardens always laid in squared furrows; but to be a creature who always thinks of two margins, left and right as the poem is being made, who believes as much in the right-hand margin as he or she does in the left, is more than a pun about politics. The business of politics is the business of discourse, and the language of discourse is prose, the language of one margin only, and that one margin, in politics, may be called right when it is left and left when it is right.

As this quotation shows, the term "discursive" should not be taken to mean "leading to reasonable conclusions" (i.e., of one margin only), but should suggest something more like its etymological meaning of "running back and forth."

6 Walcott, "As John to Patmos," in *Green Night*, 12.

7 I am grateful to Professor Shullenberger for pointing out how the poet unwrites the initial description of Patmos in this way.

8 Derek Walcott, "Guyana" (1969), in *Collected Poems 1948–1984* (New York, 1986), 115.

9 Derek Walcott, "Tales of the Islands," in *Green Night*, 26.

10 Derek Walcott, *Omeros* (New York, 1993 [1990]), 195 (5.38.2).

11 Walcott, "As John to Patmos," in *Green Night*, 12.

12 Derek Walcott, "The Estranging Sea," in *Another Life* (New York, 1973), 152. See also Matthew 5:14.

13 Walcott, "As John to Patmos," in *Green Night*, 12.

14  I do not mean to overstate the case with John. There is, to be sure, also something like love in his narrative, as when, for example, he extends his greeting to the seven churches: χάρις ὁμῖν καὶ εἰρήνη ("Grace and peace [be] to you" [1.4]), both of which depend greatly on the love of God (1.5). (All quotations in English are from *The Oxford Study Bible*, ed. M. Jack Suggs, Katharine Doob Sakenfeld, and James R. Mueller [New York, 1992].)

15  Again I thank Bill Shullenberger, who, emphasizing the quality of these rhymes, spurred me to consider their thematic implications.

16  There is also the possibility that the worker, at least, is *literally* sleeping under those red trees!

17  Walcott, "Two Poems on the Passing of an Empire," in *Green Night*, 38.

18  Derek Walcott, "Roseau Valley," in *The Arkansas Testament* (New York, 1987), 16–20.

19  The gulf between the dead and the living is effectively addressed in "Laventille," but there, unfortunately, the union of the two groups finally comes to feel like an unnatural relation, a suffocating stasis: "and in its swaddling cerements we're still bound"; Derek Walcott, "Laventille," in *The Gulf*, 16. For a discussion of this poem, see Kenneth Ramchand, "Readings of 'Laventille' [*sic*]" (1975), in *Critical Perspectives on Derek Walcott*, ed. Robert D. Hamner (Washington, 1993), 168–73.

20  Derek Walcott, "Elegy," in *Green Night*, 13.

21  Walcott, "Anadyomene," in *Green Night*, 57.

22  Walcott, "Choc Bay," in *Green Night*, 24.

23  Derek Walcott, "Origins," in *Selected Poems* (New York, 1964), 51, 53.

24  Ibid., 54–55.

25  Derek Walcott, "From This Far," in *The Fortunate Traveller* (New York, 1981), 29.

26  Ibid., 30.

Judith Harris

Giotto's Invisible Sheep: Lacanian Mirroring
and Modeling in Walcott's *Another Life*

Emerging as a poet whose West Indian cultural
identity is frozen within the ontological riddle of
the landscape, Walcott acknowledges in an autobiographical preface, "What the Twilight Says,"
that the New World poet must start from scratch:

> In that simple schizophrenic boyhood one
> could lead two lives: the interior life of poetry,
> the outward life of action and dialect. Yet the
> writers of my generation were natural assimi-
> lators. We knew the literature of Empires,
> Greek, Roman, British, through their essential
> classics; and both the patois of the street and
> the language of the classroom hid the elation
> of discovery. If there was nothing, there was
> everything to be made. With this prodigious
> ambition one began.[1]

This ambition is problematic, given the indirec-
tion of a language that can only come into being
through the presence of an other—*through* an
other. As the Lacanian model suggests, subjectivity arises with the child's entry into the Symbolic order, when he or she acquires language, a
name, and social prohibitions. Subject formation
is therefore based on assimilating a variety of ele-

The *South Atlantic Quarterly* 96:2, Spring 1997.
Copyright © 1997 by Duke University Press.

ments within one's social context, including the crucial element of difference. During Walcott's earliest apprentice years, he speculated about the confrontation of two contrasting worlds—Europe and its former colonies—and how to integrate the Western literary tradition into his provincialism without destroying his childlike sense of awe:

> Provincialism loves the pseudo-epic,
> so if these heroes have been given a stature
> disproportionate to their cramped lives,
> remember I beheld them at knee-height,
> and that their thunderous exchanges
> rumbled like gods about another life.[2]

From a psychoanalytic perspective, subject formation is a universal operation of mitigating the profound and frustrating processes involved in forming an identity. For Walcott, the notion of self/alienation is compounded by an adopted culture's language that subjects him *as it constructs him*. In phenomenological terms, the locus of identity revolves around the Other, that central presence, real or conceived, through which we become self-aware by regarding ourselves as another would. For Lacan, the subject is constantly having to remake itself in encounters with the speech that presupposes an addressee. Lacan's Other is closely associated with language itself, or at least with the *place of otherness* to which language is directed.

Walcott opens "The Divided Child," part 1 of *Another Life*, with an epigraph from Malraux's *Psychology of Art* in which Vasari's account of the lives of Cimabue and Giotto is rendered. The epigraph's obvious message is that the true artist, accepting his master's tutelage, learns to love works of art over the things they portray. Less obvious is the way in which the apprentice renders the landscape through the master's mediation, hoping to capture an art language that can mediate the world of objects. A Lacanian scheme is especially appropriate as a mode for understanding the process of artistic apprenticeship because it suggests that all language presupposes the absence of the object it signifies; hence a painting or poem refers not to the object from which it was derived (as a series of marks or articulations) but to a *prior* learned and assimilated object of art. This bears crucially on Walcott's view of every language as owing something to others, with obvious implications for art. As Walcott argues, "There is no distinction between the derivative, which has 'originat[ed] from' something, and the 'original,' from which subsequent forms derive."[3] Even the inimitable is an attempted copy that will itself be copied.

Rei Terada has demonstrated in *Derek Walcott's Poetry: American Mimicry* that Walcott views mimicry as an inescapable condition of all art, but one that the artist must use to his or her advantage. In the Cimabue and Giotto paradigm, the master is "struck" by the way in which his pupil has appropriated his own representation of the landscape. Unlike "mimesis," a representation of reality, mimicry is a "representation of a representation," something that the gifted student instinctively knows.[4] Walcott's epigraphic use of the story of Cimabue and Giotto, then, suggests a paradigm (for "The Divided Child," at least) of a hidden reciprocal relationship between master and apprentice, who mirror one another and influence each other's art. But it also suggests a parallel binary opposition in which the master/apprentice relationship is subverted in order to disrupt the hegemonic fixity of the colonizer/colonized relationship. This twofold paradigm serves as a reminder of how the West Indian apprentice in *Another Life* transcends the European master's legacy in order to begin over, subordinating the old to the tabula rasa of the new. A psychoanalytic study of racial identity in "The Divided Child" section of *Another Life* reveals Walcott's rhetorical strategy for undermining the master's vision of reality in order to interrupt and subvert that racist discourse.

If the New World Black is to be liberated from cultural servitude, Walcott suggests, it will be due to nothing less than the spawning of a new language, the reinvention of names for New World things. Growing up in the St. Lucian capital of Castries, he was steeped in classical and canonical (British) literature as well as the indigenous folktales still popular on the island. Seeking an "electric fusion of the old and the new,"[5] Walcott opens part 1 of *Another Life* with the Vasari/Malraux epigraph just described:

> An old story goes that Cimabue was struck with admiration when he saw the shepherd boy, Giotto, sketching sheep. But, according to the true biographies, it is never the sheep that inspire a Giotto with the love of painting: but, rather, his first sight of the paintings of such a man as Cimabue. What makes the artist is the circumstance that in his youth he was more deeply moved by the sight of works of art than by that of the things which they portray.

Cimabue was not aware that the boy was sketching from his own compositions when he was "struck with admiration" for Giotto, although he should not have been surprised, having once been an apprentice himself. But there was something in Giotto's drawing of the sheep that went beyond their literal representation. Cimabue, as a boy in the fourteenth century, had been sent to the monastery to study letters, but he spent most of his time drawing imaginary horses, men, and houses in his books. Later, apprenticing himself to professional painters, Cimabue modeled his style on the Greeks, but developed his own idiom.[6] An Italian master by the time he met Giotto, Cimabue then became the subject of what he saw in Giotto's *seeing* him.

The language of painting precedes and preempts the particular subject matter it represents, blinding painter and viewer alike to what is real and what is illusion. Lacan's theories of the Imaginary and of the alienation that underlies human identity postulate a similar misrecognition when the infant takes a mirror image (e.g., Giotto's sheep) as the model for self-identity, casting aside the actual conditions of an untotalized, fragmentary being (e.g., the markings of sheep). The infant's designation of the mirror image as "me" (or *moi*) comes at a developmental point when children are still incapable of controlling the actions of their bodies, and it marks a radical transformation, as the infant is basically treating an imaginary self (i.e., the imaged self, which is nonself) as one with which it must identify. Therein lies the source of alienation in the infant at the mirror stage.[7] The discordance between the inner, unintegrated experience and the external image opens a gap for a whole sequence of illusionary images that attempt to overcome self-division. Underneath the sense of spatial identity acquired by the infant who sees himself reflected in a mirror, there is the haunting recognition of a more fragmentary being. While Giotto's sheep might have seemed beautiful to Cimabue, what he appreciated more were their artistic forms. Without a prior visual language in which to record his own reading of "sheepness," the beauty of this form would not have been perceptible to Giotto's eye. He needed a starting point, a reference for symbolization as well as a desire to articulate a particular aesthetic, for both of which he was indebted to Cimabue.

Similarly, our own form is hidden from us (as the form of a drawing is concealed by its subject, e.g., sheep), and it takes *others* to make one's form evident. It is in the space of the Other that the subject comes to see himself, a psychological and perceptual dynamic that informs Walcott's thinking about the simulations involved in constructing West Indian identity. The mimic needs a mirror in which to see himself in relation to the one he aims to imitate. Cimabue's admiration for what he saw through Giotto enabled him to see a reflection of his own painterly signature. Although he probably did not realize it, Cimabue invested narcissistic libido in his reading of Giotto's work. Narcissism is not solipsistic but has a social dimension, needing an Other to model itself on, to impress, or respond to.[8] Alternative versions of the Cimabue/Giotto meeting might mislead us into believing that Cimabue was entranced by the beauty of Giotto's sheep; more remarkable is the fact that we conceal from ourselves what is an artifice and what is real.

Giotto's rendering of sheep was of what Cimabue saw: *invisible* objects, which provide the ground for the Imaginary. Perhaps Cimabue did not even know he *desired* that appreciation for beauty until he saw it revived through the work of his most gifted student. In *Another Life*, Walcott tried to touch the essence of his native island, as Giotto was trying to touch sheep, but reality is always mediated by language, and, as Lacan suggests, no autonomous self can transcend it. While memory cannot (and should not) erase the past, the shackles of mastery can only be broken by a revelation of the future grasped through the language that claims it. Out of an indigenous idiom, Walcott has crafted a new culture and language for the islands, eliciting what Emerson called Naming in the highest sense.[9] Or, as Walcott quotes Alejo Carpentier as saying in *The Lost Steps*: "The only task appropriate to the milieu that was slowly revealing to me the nature of its values [was] Adam's task of giving things their names."[10]

In "Homage to Gregorias" (part 2 of *Another Life*), Walcott distinguishes his evolving art or aesthetic from that of a painter he calls Gregorias, contrasting his own classicism to the painter's romanticism:

> While Gregorias would draw
> with the linear elation of an eel
> one muscle in one thought,
> my hand was crabbed by that style
>
> . . . .
>
> it was classic versus romantic
> perhaps, it was water and fire.[11]

When Walcott tried to "render the visible world" in brushstrokes, he was prone to see the world through subtle metaphors and paradoxes that more properly belonged to a literary tradition. Due to his mixed heritage, he saw the island as "a crystal of ambiguities," including translations from the colonizer's language. While Gregorias's style was marked by an "aboriginal force" that, inborn, burst through "as the carver comes out of the wood," Walcott's poetry was servile, subdued by a classical training that he likens to the crab's "sidewise crawling." Walcott's self-deprecatory "crabness" suggests a nebulous mixture of influences as well as a myopic, defensive stance. But what made Gregorias so admirable was his courage in discarding traditional Western aesthetics and making "grotesque" images in order to forge an art that was wholly his own. Walcott, on the other hand, modeled his aesthetic on the one he found in his "father's small blue library / of reproductions . . . / . . . and in another / sky-blue book / the shepherdesses of Boucher and Fragonard." Seduced by the dazzling splendors of Western masters, especially their radiant depictions of shepherdesses, as "if they were [his] Muse," Walcott interpreted his world through them, while "Gregorias bent to his handful of earth, / his black nudes gleaming sweat, / in the tiger shade of the fronds." In response to his friend's love of Western art, Gregorias observes: "The thing is you love death and I love life / Your poetry too full of spiders, / bones, worms, ants, things eating up each other." [12]

Yet Walcott's definition of "apprenticeship," which Gregorias "abandoned . . . / to the errors of his own soul," must account for, rather than eschew, the very same complexities that he has detected in the scene of Cimabue's instruction of Giotto (which was actually Giotto's instruction of Cimabue). Walcott knows that Giotto was concerned not with painting "real" sheep but with capturing painterly images of "sheepness." Mimicry is unavoidable for the West Indian artist, among others, since there is no true origination but only simulation. Gregorias's attempt to discard tradition by embracing a primitivist aesthetic does not make him immune to European influence. Walcott implies that even his landscapes and "black nudes" are derivative, reverential toward Italian painting, with "every brushstroke a prayer / to Giotto, to Masaccio / his primitive, companionable saints." [13] Gregorias's struggle is no different from that of previous Western artists, who also strove to repossess the world in terms of their own earth, their own heaven. Such is Gregorias's victory, however, that "now, every landscape we entered / was already signed with his name." But perhaps Gregorias's derision of the formalism that Walcott attempted to *master* became a kind of contamination: "Never such faith again, never such innocence!"[14] As foil to Gregorias, Walcott comes to see himself as a Promethean firebrand who steals from the Western gods, or classics, to provide for his own native tradition. As a result, he synthesizes both aspects of his heritage, combining high eloquence with touches of vernacular, stripping away glazed layers of the past in order to regain that "virginal, unpainted world" of the islands.[15] Although Walcott envisions a return to origins, ontological instability divides the self. As Helen Vendler noted in "Poet of Two Worlds":

> Walcott's agenda gradually shaped itself. He would not give up the paternal patois; he would not give up his patois to write only in formal English. He would not give up his topic—his geographical place, his historical time, and his mixed blood; neither would he give up aesthetic balance. He was in all things "a divided child" loyal to "the stuffed dark nightingale of Keats" and "the virginal unpainted world" of the islands.[16]

Walcott is alert to the otherness within, but also to the other *as other*, consistent with Lacanian subject formation's being based on the recognition of difference as determinative of personal identity. Moreover, this is consistent with Frantz Fanon's demonstration of how race fundamentally constructs and divides black identity as well. Just as a child's visual perception structures sexual difference, forcing a recognition of a lack which is then internalized, "not only must the black man be black but he must be black in relation to the white man."[17] Seeing himself fixed through the gaze of the Other, Fanon suggests that the self-divided Black child deflects what Whiteness has projected upon him, but the internalized complex of racial inferiority must be exposed for what it is so that the individual can be in a position to choose action with respect to the actual cause of the conflict—the social structure. The White man's gaze constructs and subjugates the Other. Walcott's "Divided Child" is a rare exemplar of how subjectivity is permeated by the social discourse that has preceded and constructed it to such an extent that the child acquires a "double" image of the self. Desire is poignantly expressed as the need to be recognized by an/Other, even if that Otherness is seemingly self-embodied. When the colonial sees his own disfigured child, it is as an abomination that he rejects, forgetting that it was he who created him in the first place *and in his own image*: "The dream / of reason had produced its monster: / a prodigy of the wrong age and colour."[18] To speak is "to exist absolutely for the other,"[19] suggests Fanon. Indeed, Walcott's mixed racial origins divide his loyalties, a theme taken up as early as 1962, in "A Far Cry from Africa." The last—and frequently quoted—stanza of this poem foregrounds not only race but also language, setting the physical beauty of the landscape against the authoritative "tongue" the speaker loves:

> I who am poisoned with the blood of both,
> Where shall I turn, divided to the vein?
> I who have cursed
> The drunken officer of British rule, how choose
> Between this Africa and the English tongue I love?[20]

Postcolonial history still belongs to conquerors who imposed their languages on other peoples and who continue to dominate their writing. Walcott "entered the house of literature as a houseboy,"[21] doting on a reliquary of Victorian heirlooms. But his love for the English tongue did not preclude his expressing moral outrage over the crimes of the epoch, reminding us that "death rattles in every room" of the English mansion and that the muteness of the colonized is a silent scream.[22] In "Gros-Ilet," Walcott describes a "village, soaked like a grey rag in salt water," from which

> a language came, garnished with conch-shells,
> with a suspicion of berries in its armpits
> and elbows like flexible oars. . . .
>
> . . . .
>
> There are different candles and customs here, the dead
> are different. Different shells guard their graves.
> There are distinctions even beyond the paradise
> of the horizon. This is not the grape-purple Aegean.
> There is no wine here, no cheese, the almonds are green,
> the sea-grapes bitter, the language is that of slaves.[23]

Civilization has substituted heaven for a primitive horizon; it has framed the New World in what the boy of *Another Life* attributes to "other men's voices / other men's lives and lines."[24] The natives now sleep as if dead, giving up their dreams to a nostalgic *idea* of Western paradise. The language they have mastered now enslaves them. Western art is coveted and collected by the boy's father: "that fine drawn hare of Dürer's, clenched and quivering / to leap across my wrist. . . . / . . . Peter de Wint, Paul Sandby, Cotman."[25] But if the colonizer has *imposed* his history on the unpainted landscape, Walcott subverts this schema by turning the apprentice into the master, the beauty of his speech transfiguring the local people, making them heroes from the Old World and its myths: "These dead, these derelicts, / that alphabet of the emaciated, / they were the stars of my mythology."[26] Now the master must read his art through the student's inspired reading of him. Hence Walcott's Castries becomes Troy; his city, the New Jerusalem; his drunken painter friend Dunstan St. Omer, a Gregorias elevated to a civilizing papal figure.

"The Divided Child" begins with the boy finishing a sketch of the harbor for a critique by his art teacher (Harry Simmons). The point of view is the boy's, which lends a sense of immediacy, but this perspective is also enriched by the more pervasive reflections of the older narrator's longer view.[27] Here, a narcissistic gaze mirrors the Self through an Other, as Cimabue saw himself through Giotto, birthing a double consciousness:

> Verandahs, where the pages of the sea
> are a book left open by an absent master
> in the middle of another life—
> I begin here again,
> begin until this ocean's
> a shut book, and like a bulb
> the white moon's filaments wane.
>
> Begin with twilight, when a glare
> which held a cry of bugles lowered
> the coconut lances of the inlet,
> as a sun, tired of empire, declined.
> . . . .
>             There
> was your heaven! The clear
> glaze of another life,
> a landscape locked in amber, the rare
> gleam.[28]

In "the clear / glaze of another life," a tribal order is frozen in amber—and in the English word *amber*. But "the rare / gleam" shoots through, prefiguring Walcott's mature vision of Genesis, a regenerative motif that, in the title poem of *The Star-Apple Kingdom*, roots the history of the Caribbean in one Black woman who sees "the creak of light" that divided the world suddenly dissolve into "the white, silent roar / of the old water wheel in the star-apple kingdom."[29]

As the boy of "The Divided Child" looks out over the harbor, he is eager to finish the sketch before the natural light fades. Light, its intensities and shadows, glazes the scene as it "completes itself" in the darkness, becoming what it is even as it becomes invisible. The apprentice must navigate around the obstacles that intrude on the scene, his mind reeling with images of latter-day legions and the colonial empire: "the gables of the St. Antoine Hotel / aspiring from jungle, the flag / at Government House melting its pole." In fact, the vision cannot be sustained *without* the boy's integrating the imperialist apparatus into the familiar scene, with "the last shacks" "transfigured" as "a cinquecento fragment in gilt frame."[30]

Poets are natural assimilators, but, unlike artists, they are removed from the triggering subject by a preposition: one writes *of* or *about* something. The poet's challenge is to link himself with his subject.[31] In the opening lines of "The Divided Child," we are told that a book is "left open by an absent master / in the middle of another life" and that the apprentice must "begin here again." Whether the master be Our-Father-Who-Art-in-Heaven or "Our father, / who floated in the vaults of Michelangelo,"[32] or the dead father who is the absent presence in the childhood house, the master artist has become distracted, leaving an opening for the apprentice, who will adapt the master's vision of reality in the interest of his own tutelage. Each master's "reading" of the world is supplemented by an Other's, which continually destabilizes the fixity of hierarchical positions.

As twilight settles on the landscape, the fledgling artist sees the hills "simplified" and turned to "hunks of coal." But the painter's task is to see beyond use or even colonial exploitation, to retain an aesthetic distance, however self/betraying and self/divisive. As "the moon maintain[s] her station," shipwrecked relics—"antique furniture"—and cheap reproductions of European art are exposed in all their decadence:

> the mantel
> with its plaster-of-Paris Venus, which

> his yearning had made marble, half-cracked
> unsilvering mirror of black servants,
> like the painter's kerchiefed, ear-ringed portrait: Albertina.[33]

Pastoral munificence squandered by European landlords is now evident in the lunar reflections of a servile and "barefooted town." The moon's "sign" is "a dry park of disconsolate palms, like brooms, / planted by the Seventh Edward, Prince of Wales, / with drooping ostrich crests, ICH DIEN, I SERVE."[34]

Framed within the Westerner's primitive picturesque, culture gives birth to its reader. The mind of the painting teacher is haloed, a tonsure encircled by light, "crouched / in its pale tissue like an embryo." As the sketch is finally offered for critique and the teacher modifies the student's strokes according to his own reason and reference, the student becomes aware of yet another interloper: the secondhand nature of an already-limited visual language: "In its dimension the drawing could not trace / the sociological contours of the promontory."[35] Art can only allude to political realities:

> The groves were sawn
>
> . . . .
>
> down the arched barrack balconies
> where colonels in the whisky-coloured light
> had watched the green flash, like a lizard's tongue,
> catch the last sail.[36]

More significant here is the disoriented moon, a symbol of third-person consciousness. Feminized, she is the light that brings objects to the surface, but while she dominates the black sky, the boy, "her subject," desires to be the object of her desire, which is to be White: "from childhood he'd considered palms / ignobler than imagined elms," and "he had prayed / nightly for his flesh to change, / his dun flesh peeled white by her lightning strokes!"[37] Here, the boy's image is self-rejected, "whitewashed" by a love for another life: "a moon ballooned. . . . O / mirror, where a generation *yearned / for whiteness*, for candour, unreturned. // The moon . . . / . . . whitewashed the shells."[38] The boy's desire is unconscious, for the child's first desire is *to be* the desire of the m(Other). To be desired is to be precipitated forward by language, which stands for one's lack of *being* that desired object. Lacan suggests that what we seek in the Other (an/other) is some recognition of ourselves as desiring subjects outside language, of our identities as not entirely awash in the constructions of our fantasies.[39] Hence the boy's language expresses his town's futile wish to be seen positively through the counterfeit gaze of the white moon, to which these towns-people have no "ontological resistance" (as Fanon would say) and without which they would seem not to exist: "Well, everything whitens, / all that town's characters, its cast of thousands," for "their flesh [is] like flaking stone, / poor negatives!"[40]

The moon's "white face" also invites associations with the variously masked ventriloquist, mime, and satirical minstrel. Through his ventrilo-quistic and satiric deployment of European influences (which, he contends, cannot be extracted from his native tradition), Walcott aesthetically destabi-lizes political categories without having to acknowledge history's molding of poetic form or content. Even for "the divided child," who has not yet been initiated into the complexities of racial identity, the white moon is an illusion, "her" light deceptive, a mocking night sun at the studio window. "She" reads the world below from "her" privileged position, but is far-sighted, seeing what is close as distant, mirroring the unbridgeable chasm between the boy's myopic identifications, as "her slow disc magnified / the life beneath her like a reading-glass." The "master's" book that opened the poem is echoed by the painter's "green book, laid / face downward. Moon, / and sea. He read / the spine. FIRST POEMS: / CAMPBELL." Reading, "the painter / almost absently / reversed it," as all things seem reversed by dialectical relations:

> Holy be
> the white head of a Negro,
> sacred be
> the black flax of a black child.[41]

The whitehaired Black master is patronized; the apprentice must assume his position in a certain line, but, by accepting one tradition, he betrays the other. The Scottish poet's book that elicits such enthusiasm from the boy is "bound in sea-green linen" by a colonized people and from their natu-ral resources. The boy's self-estrangement seems permanent: "the white face / of a dead child stared from its window-frame."[42] Here the child re-veals a primal fear of what has been repressed all this time: death, like the Real, is the "impossible" core of human identity. (As Jonathan Lee notes, Lacan characterizes the Real as "the mystery of the speaking body," or the unconscious; it is what stands behind the reality constituted in and by our use of language, only hinting at its presence through the failures and ruptures that mark this symbolic system.[43]) Walcott's embrace of cultural amnesia may be a gesture toward this mystery of an unconscious that is continually in motion, continually reborn.

The European literary model is indispensable to Walcott's poetry, but so is his native heritage. Out of both his childhood memories and his racial memory comes an imaginative drive "to praise lovelong, the living and the brown dead" of his island,[44] to interpret what that society sees. Walcott's intent in *Another Life* is to *reverse* the perceptual order, to reinterpret the history of the islands by painting over (whiting out) received narratives with fresh discursive colors and glazes. Although he has been criticized for not explicitly taking a revolutionary stance within the Caribbean culture wars, it can be argued that he is effectively doing so by consciously or unconsciously depicting himself as the revolutionary apprentice who rebels against—and surpasses—the colonial master's style and determinative influence. Reacting in 1971 to charges that he mimicked the master's language and literature, Walcott said:

> A great amount of the Third World literature is a literature of revenge written by the descendants of slaves bent on exorcising this demon [history] through the word. Or a literature of remorse written by the descendants of masters obsessed by guilt. . . . The truly classic—written by those who practice the tough aesthetic of the New World—neither explains nor forgives history because it refuses to recognize it as a creative force. . . . The old style Revolutionary Writer sees Caliban as an enraged pupil. He can't separate the rage of Caliban from the beauty of his speech. . . . The language of the torturer has been mastered by the victim. Yet this is viewed as servitude, not as irony or victory![45]

Walcott's appropriation of the "heiratic objects" of European art in *Another Life* reveals his love for Caliban's eloquence, however "classical" a character he may be. While the goal of a back-to-Africa movement is to purge the colonial influence, the movement itself, according to Walcott, is mimicking something that does not exist except in the White colonialist's imagination, a lesson he learned early on, like the boy in *Another Life* who spurns his dead father's artworks, "venerable objects / borne by . . . black hands," and yearns for an ancestry of "the deep country," or the bush. However, he discovers that this "natural man" for whom he is searching is merely an illusion, one of colonialism's constructs.[46]

Mimicry is therefore an aesthetic concept for Walcott, one that he appropriates and cultivates in positive terms. As Terada aptly demonstrates, mimicry is the very ground for Walcott's creative revolution: "Mimicry, with all its ambivalent freight, replaces mimesis as the ground of representation and culture."[47] As Terada also points out, mimicry redefines itself through the lens of postmodernism, which has questioned the idea of originality, or the existence of a starting point, and has emphasized the secondariness of a signifying chain. In "The Caribbean: Culture or Mimicry?" Walcott asserts that once "the meridian of European civilization has been crossed," there is no longer any point of origination, for "the cord is cut by that meridian."[48] Lacan makes the same assertion with regard to language: entering the Symbolic means being severed (or cut off) from the Imaginary, or body of origination, which can only be recaptured through the substitute of a transitory utterance.[49]

Gregorias's return to aboriginal roots, then, is impossible: "We cannot return to what we have never been."[50] With nothing more than the earth to believe in, the boy in *Another Life* is brought back to the soil as an end point *and* a starting point. Walcott insists that the West Indian must have a vision of him- or herself that more closely corresponds to what he or she is *now* rather than to where he or she came from.[51] With nothing to begin with, there is "everything to be made," as Walcott says.[52] This is an affirming gesture, better and deeper than one of despair.

The act of beginning is always language's beginning, for language fails only to end itself. "There is no beginning but no end," as Walcott states in "The Muse of History": "The new poet enters a flux and withdraws, as the weaver continues the pattern, hand to hand."[53] What Giotto saw as great in Cimabue was both the past and the future, and what Cimabue saw in Giotto was what he did not think he would see himself—the dawning of the Renaissance. Significantly, *Another Life* concludes with the poet's declaration of art's power to rename the postcolonial world. Returning to the image of the painter Gregorias, Walcott shows him sketching "the smooth white walls of clouds and villages" *over an underpainting* by the master. In Gregorias's "impossible" yet "inexhaustible" Renaissance, "brown cherubs of Giotto and Masaccio" mingle with an incongruous "salt wind . . . / smelling of turpentine, with nothing so old / that it could not be invented." [54] By the end, the sleep of history must be wiped away, the eyes of the dead master's unfinished portraits "blown out." The artist, liberated, can begin to construct a new sequence.

The polarizations of the self-divided child are rooted in discourse and, here, complicated by racial difference. Memory is as fixed as any object, and as easily lost. Although the object may be gone, however, it will not be abandoned: language is wrought by shaping words, as an object is shaped by the hand that it hollows. The poet, like the still-life painter, persists in finding "the rightness of placed things." [55] For Walcott, this prior positioning depends on the effort to recreate it, although there is always that misalignment between reality and reflection. In painting, lines delineate the edges between things, edges which in reality do not exist, as Walcott himself observes: "There are already, invisible on canvas, / lines locking into outlines. The visible dissolves / in a benign acid." [56] A line in painting has extension but no dimension. No such lines exist in nature. Cimabue, the master, read Giotto's line in the mirror of his own reference, one that Giotto *mastered* in order to copy Cimabue. Walcott's poetic line likewise mirrors his own models, both dividing and connecting his two worlds.

**Notes**

I would like to thank Marshall W. Alcorn for inspiring this essay, and Gregson Davis for his guidance.

1   Derek Walcott, "What the Twilight Says: An Overture," in *Dream on Monkey Mountain and Other Plays* (New York, 1970), 3–40; quotation from 4. See also David Mason, "Derek Walcott, Poet of the New World," *Literary Review* 29 (1986): 269–75, esp. 269.

2   Derek Walcott, "The Divided Child," in *Another Life* (New York, 1973), 41. See also Edward Baugh, *Derek Walcott: Memory as Vision* (London, 1978), 81.

3   Quoted in Rei Terada, *Derek Walcott's Poetry: American Mimicry* (Boston, 1992), 24.

4   Ibid., 1.

5   Robert D. Hamner, "Derek Walcott," in *Critical Survey of Poetry*, Vol. 7, ed. Frank Magill (Englewood Cliffs, 1982), 3003.

6   On Cimabue, see Monica Chellini, *Cimabue* (Florence and New York, 1988).

7   See Jonathan Scott Lee, *Jacques Lacan* (Boston, 1990), 18.

8   See Marshall W. Alcorn, Jr., *Narcissism and the Literary Libido: Rhetoric, Text, and Subjectivity* (New York, 1994), 16.

9   Peter Balakian, "The Poetry of Derek Walcott," *Poetry* 147 (1986): 169–77; quotation from 170.

10   Walcott, "Homage to Gregorias," in *Another Life*, 47.

11  Ibid., 59.

12  Ibid., 59, 60, 61, 64.

13  Ibid., 59, 61.

14  Ibid., 59, 61.

15  Walcott, "The Estranging Sea," in *Another Life*, 152.

16  Quoted in Mason, "Derek Walcott," 271.

17  Frantz Fanon, *Black Skin, White Masks*, trans. Charles Lam Markmann (New York, 1991 [1967]), 110.

18  Walcott, "The Divided Child," 3.

19  Fanon, *Black Skin, White Masks*, 17.

20  Derek Walcott, "A Far Cry from Africa," in *Collected Poems 1948–1984* (New York, 1986), 17.

21  Walcott, "Homage to Gregorias," 77.

22  See Balakian, "Poetry of Derek Walcott," 175.

23  Derek Walcott, "Gros-Ilet," *Literary Review* 29 (1986): 256.

24  Walcott, "A Simple Flame," in *Another Life*, 106.

25  Walcott, "Homage to Gregorias," 60.

26  Walcott, "The Divided Child," 22.

27  See Baugh, *Derek Walcott*, 80.

28  Walcott, "The Divided Child," 3.

29  Derek Walcott, "The Star-Apple Kingdom," in *Collected Poems*, 395.

30  Walcott, "The Divided Child," 4.

31  Cf. Robert Bensen, "The Painter as Poet: Derek Walcott's *Midsummer*," *Literary Review* 29 (1986): 257–68, esp. 266.

32  Walcott, "The Divided Child," 3, 44.

33  Ibid., 5.

34  Ibid., 10.

35  Ibid., 5, 6.

36  Ibid., 6.

37  Ibid., 6, 7.

38  Ibid., 4–5; my emphasis.

39  See Lee, *Jacques Lacan*, 67.

40  Walcott, "The Divided Child," 9.

41  Ibid., 7.

42  Ibid.

43  Lee, *Jacques Lacan*, 136.

44  Derek Walcott, "As John to Patmos," in *In A Green Night: Poems 1948–1960* (London, 1962), 12.

45  Quoted in Baugh, *Derek Walcott*, 86.

46  Walcott, "The Divided Child," 42; see also 43.

47  Terada, *Derek Walcott's Poetry*, 2.

48  Quoted in ibid., 22.

49  See Terry Eagleton, *Literary Theory: An Introduction* (Minneapolis, 1983), 168.

50  Terada, *Derek Walcott's Poetry*, 22.

51  See Baugh, *Derek Walcott*, 67.

52  Walcott, "What the Twilight Says," 4.

53  Quoted in Terada, *Derek Walcott's Poetry*, 43.

54  Walcott, "The Estranging Sea," 152.

55  Walcott, "The Divided Child," 15.

56  Walcott, "Homage to Gregorias," 55.

**Edward Baugh**

# The Poet's Fiction of Self:
## "The Schooner *Flight*"

Derek Walcott's poetry constitutes an ongoing fiction of himself, and "The Schooner *Flight*" is a definitive embodiment of this idea and a landmark moment in this process. As I have said elsewhere, "Walcott's binding theme is Walcott, the pursuit and delineation of a fictive character based on an actual person named Derek Walcott."[1] This writing of the self involves a process of self-address and self-interrogation. No mere egocentricity or self-indulgent display of private angst, it is Walcott's way of engaging with the world, by examining himself-in-the-world. The general sense in which the poet enters the fictive construct and unfolding story that is his poetry is instanced, for example, by the way in which he enters, as a character, the particular narrative/fiction *Omeros*.

The narrator/protagonist of "The Schooner *Flight*," a mulatto sailor/poet identified only by his nickname, Shabine, tells of how he slipped secretly from Trinidad, his island domicile, early one morning "to ship as a seaman on the schooner *Flight*."[2] His reasons for leaving the island, which it grieved him to do, were both public and private. On the one hand, he had

The *South Atlantic Quarterly* 96:2, Spring 1997.
Copyright © 1997 by Duke University Press.

become disillusioned and bitter over the condition of society—the corruption of values and of politics—and over his own ensnarement in that corruption. On the other hand, he was being torn apart by a dilemma of the heart, torn between love of wife and love of mistress. He then recounts some of his experiences on his outward voyage and the feelings and thoughts attaching to those experiences, from which we learn something about his earlier life. The *Flight* passes Blanchisseuse in Trinidad, as well as Barbados and Dominica, and anchors in Castries harbor. This geographical maneuver enables the poem to take in the West Indies as a whole and allows Shabine's imagination to voyage backward into West Indian history, for example, to the destruction of the aboriginal Caribs and the horrors of the Middle Passage. The narrative builds to a climax when a storm almost destroys the schooner and its crew. Shabine, coming out of the experience at peace with himself and the world, invokes a blessing on the islands. The poem ends with him sailing on, to no definite destination, although it may end more ambiguously, with the last line indicating that the voice of Shabine is the voice of a drowned sailor. In any event, he has given us a summary of his life, and a self-portrait.

The poet's constructing himself as a character in the fiction that is his poetry is related to his lifelong interest in the relationship between genres and modes, to his experimentation with their interplay and fusion. A major, pathfinding example is *Another Life* (1973), the poem that is also a novel and an autobiography. This work not only marked an important development in Walcott's (re-)appropriating for poetry certain qualities of prose fiction; writing it also provoked a searching engagement with the idea of autobiography. In the original manuscript from which *Another Life* emerged, having started out as an intended prose memoir, we find him theorizing on the nature of autobiography and on the relationships and differences among autobiography, travel writing, novel, and poetry. It was only natural in the circumstances that he should have reflected on autobiography—as if, finding himself drawn into the apparent self-indulgence of that genre to which he had not aspired—he felt a need to reflect on the direction he seemed to be taking. It is significant that autobiography was what sparked his reflections on genre, mode, voice; for it may be seen as the mode that mediates between the more subjective/lyric voice and the more impersonal/narrative voice. Indeed, Walcott sees all genres as modes of autobiography: "Those who have abandoned poetry for other forms of autobiography like fiction, the long essay and the travel book will remain split down the middle, petrified and Janus-headed."[3]

At the same time, autobiography is a form of fiction:

> All autobiographies should be in the third person. The pretext of confession, whose real purpose is not exploring but ennobling life, is the supreme fiction. . . . So the lie, once we have created this trance of style, of finding progress and illumination where there was really luck or repetition, multiplies once we begin. Henceforth "I" should be known as "him"—an object distant enough to regard dispassionately. . . . The true autobiographer will cultivate the schizophrenic gift.[4]

Walcott is himself an assiduous cultivator of this "gift." For instance, in *Another Life*, where his awareness of it first came into sharp focus, the pronominal identification of the narrator/protagonist keeps shifting among first, second, and third person to enact the drama of autobiography, indeed, of writing, as a form of self-address and self-interrogation.

Stephen Spender offers another view of the necessary "schizophrenia" of the autobiographer when he says, "An autobiographer is really writing a story of two lives: his life as it appears to himself, from his own position, when he looks out at the world from behind his eye-sockets; and his life as it appears from outside in the minds of others; a view which tends to become in part his own view of himself also, since he is influenced by the opinion of those others."[5] Walcott is keenly aware of the tension between the subjective, suffering, perceiving "I" and the objective "I"/"him," which is other. This tension arises from the uncertainty of distinguishing between the two and ends in the awareness that the writer—whether novelist or poet or autobiographer, all being makers of fictions—"creates" his life in the process of writing about it. The writing, then, enacts the notion, attributed by Malcolm Lowry to José Ortega y Gasset, that "a man's life is like a fiction that he makes up as he goes along."[6] This idea is no doubt more manifest in the work of some writers than in that of others. It seems appropriate that it should have been seized upon approvingly by Lowry, whose own work is a fictionalizing of his life.

Similarly with Walcott: we may regard his work as a whole, including the plays to varying degrees, as one continuing fiction, a story whose protagonist is the poet persona, a "character" who is gradually being discovered and created through various metamorphoses, contradictions, and continuities, but who is not necessarily recognizable at any given moment as the Walcott one might meet in the flesh. By this process of self-creation, which is simultaneously a process of self-discovery, the man who is living from day to day his inchoate existence imposes a kind of order on it and creates his personal myth, so to speak: the conceptual framework within which to make sense of his existence. As John Cowper Powys remarked in reference to his own *Autobiography*, "A person's life-illusion ought to be as sacred as his skin."[7] Also relevant here is Thom Gunn's "theory of pose," which he "based partly on the dramatics of John Donne, somewhat perhaps on Yeats's theory of masks, and most strongly on the behaviour of Stendhal's heroes. . . . The theory of pose was this: everyone plays a part, whether he knows it or not, so he might as well deliberately design a part, or a series of parts, for himself."[8]

The idea of the fiction of self, of one's life and/or writing as a striving toward the realization of one's idea of oneself, not only informs much of Walcott's poetry, but is explicitly stated in some of his characterizations. For example, in *Another Life*, after sketching some of the interesting minor figures of the world of his childhood, he sums up: "Baron, ship-chandler, merchant, water-clerk, / the fiction of their own lives claimed each one."[9] In "Koenig of the River," Koenig becomes aware of himself as a character out of fiction: "he felt bodiless, like a man stumbling from / the pages of a novel, not a forest, / written a hundred years ago." Then he begins to realize that he controls this fiction, that he is king not of the river but of the idea of himself: "If I'm a character called Koenig, then I / shall dominate my future like a fiction / in which there is a real river and real sky."[10] He too is being "claimed" by the fiction of himself. So is Sonora, "the socialist," the would-be revolutionary who "for a straight double-rum . . . / on any given Sunday / will narrate [his] adventure, which, inevitably, / a loss of heredity needs to create."[11] For such as Sonora, fiction has degenerated into fantasy, a professional hazard for all fictions of self, as the literary efforts of V. S. Naipaul's Jimmy Ahmed, the protagonist of *Guerrillas*, well illustrate.

Through the variations of the Walcott persona, the idea of the life as an unfolding narrative that gives it shape and significance is underscored by the fact that the persona not only looks backward at times, as in *Another Life*, to confront the idea of the young self from whom he has evolved, but also projects an image and idea of a future self into whom he thinks or hopes he is growing. Some characteristic features of that image are described in *Another Life*:

Anna, I wanted to grow white-haired
as the wave, with a wrinkled

brown rock's face, salted,
seamed, an old poet,
facing the wind

and nothing, which is,
the loud world in his mind.[12]

James Coburn, playing the lead in "The Man Who Loved Islands," is a variation on this ideal, with "his tanned, leathery, frail / resilience and his now whitening hair, / and his white, vicious grin."[13]

In *Midsummer*, past and future images of the self neatly cohere in a moment that encompasses the whole narrative of the life:

Sometimes the flash is seen, a sudden exultation
of lightning fixing earth in its place; the asphalt's skin
smells freshly of childhood in the drying rain.
Then I believe that it is still possible, the happiness
of truth, and the young poet who stands in the mirror
smiles with a nod. He looks beautiful from this distance.
And I hope I am what he saw, an enduring ruin.[14]

*Midsummer* is itself a version of the fiction of self, never mind its explicit lyric-meditative mode. And when, in poem XXIX, the speaker punningly refers to *Midsummer* as "leaves that keep trying to summarize [his] life,"[15] we recognize, under the whimsy, a significant definition of Walcott's entire output.

The imagery of mirror and reflection recurs, conveying, among other things, the idea of the self in self-confrontation, the drama of self as I-and-you/him, and therefore the larger notion of the fiction and narrative of self:

Time cuts down on the length man can endure
his own reflection. Entering a glass
I surface quickly now. . . .
                    Only tyrants believe
their mirrors, or Narcissi, brooding on boards,
before they plunge into their images. . . .[16]

Thus does Shabine, beginning his journey in "The Schooner *Flight*," which is at once escape, immersion, and journey toward the self, confront his reflection in the taxi's rearview mirror. Walcott thereby establishes, conceptually and structurally, a creative tension between the subjective, perceiving "I" and the "I" as other, as "him," the one whose story the former "I" is inventing: "And I look in the rearview and see a man / exactly like me, and the man was weeping / for the houses, the streets, that whole fucking island."[17] The image of Shabine looking into the rearview mirror *contains* the ideas of motion, narrative, the backward glance by a self moving forward in time and space—the idea of a fiction that aims to comprehend a life. The device of confronting the mirror image as "other" effects a certain aesthetic, ironic distancing, which minimizes the risk of too raw or sentimental an utterance of feeling and allows the poet a wider scope for maneuvering. The calypso line "with himself as chairman investigating himself,"[18] used to satirize the corrupt Establishment, represents the perversion of the poem's otherwise serious mode of perception and discourse.

Shabine, then, in expressing and at the same time investigating himself, in constructing himself through his story of himself, is a reflection of the poet (as Shabine is himself a poet), expressing and investigating himself through the story of Shabine. By means of the mask and dramatic monologue of this "red nigger who love the sea," who "had a sound colonial education," and who has "Dutch, nigger, and English in [him]," Walcott effects a fresh rehearsal of his poetic odyssey. When, after a fight with another crew member who mocked his poetry, Shabine declares decisively, "None of them go fuck with my poetry again," part of the amusement for the reader is the sense of Walcott's own sidewise swipe at his critics here. (Also like Walcott, Shabine can recall when he was "a child in the Methodist chapel / in Chisel Street, Castries," and it is significant that "The Schooner *Flight*" was written during the period when Walcott decided— apparently under trying circumstances—to leave Trinidad to work in the United States.) Shabine asks, "Where is . . . / the window I can look from that frames my life?"[19] The poem itself is one frame, conferring structure, coherence, meaning. Shabine, seeking to "frame" his life, is Walcott seeking to "summarize" *his* life. To frame one's life is to *compose* it, to invest it with the truth of art. The figure looking out of the window will be looking out on his life, which is the world, as framed by the window. At the same time, the figure is framed in the window, for the world to see.

The idea of the odyssey that informs "The Schooner *Flight*" is itself definitive and of structural significance. It invokes a whole tradition of narrative, as well as Walcott's entire career, which Lloyd Brown appropriately describes as an odyssey.[20] Walcott's poetry has been haunted by Homer's *Odyssey*—largely by way of Joyce's *Ulysses*—and behind it the *Iliad*. In the title poem of *Sea Grapes*, for example, the poet persona sees himself as an Odysseus, forever restless, forever adventuring, torn between passion and duty. *In A Green Night* maps Walcott's mythology of archipelagoes, his "litany of islands" in a sunstruck sea, islands threaded by the "needles" (masts) "of strait-stitching schooners."[21] And "The Schooner *Flight*" depicts the doughty sailors and fishermen earning their manhood in the ancient love affair and quarrel with the sea "that kills them," the ceaseless wandering and yearning—"the bowsprit, the arrow, the longing, the lunging heart"[22]—that is made to belong as naturally to Walcott's Caribbean as to Homer's Aegean. All the Odyssean notions adrift on the sea of Walcott's work inform Shabine's fiction, which is his self-portrait, but it was after "The Schooner *Flight*" that Walcott's involvement with Homer culminated in the roughly simultaneous appearance of *Omeros* and *The Odyssey: A Stage Version*. (Incidentally, the name "Flight" provides a nice instance of a detail transmuted from autobiography: one of the schooners known to Walcott in his youth in Castries was named *Flight*, which is mentioned, along with a sister vessel, *Phyllis*, in "A Sea-Chantey.")

Shabine's narrative self-quest is also comprehensive and definitive in that it draws together the various genres, forms, modes, and styles that Walcott has incorporated in his poetic odyssey. That Shabine is also a poet clinches the analogy with Walcott, on the one hand, and with Odysseus, on the other. For Odysseus was a man of wit and words; if not a poet, a man of craft, so to speak, nonetheless. And Walcott, if not a sailor, is a poet of the sea if ever there was one. When Shabine says at the end of the poem, "My first friend was the sea. Now, is my last,"[23] he speaks from behind a mask that Walcott would be comfortable wearing. Shabine's poetic affiliations justify the more lyrical flights of his monologue in terms of his characterization. That lyricism adds a fitting dimension to a narrative which is as much about Shabine's (or Walcott's) feelings about things and events as it is about those things and events in their own right, but the lyricism never works against the narrative. Even where whole sections are in the lyric mode—such as 4 ("The *Flight* Passing Blanchisseuse"), 6 ("The Sailor Sings Back to the Casuarinas"), and 7 ("The *Flight* Anchors in Castries Harbor")—and can stand alone and out of context as self-contained lyrics, part of their poignancy derives from the reader's awareness of the narrative thrust behind them. Even at moments of lyrical celebration, the landscapes or persons celebrated are being left behind in the inexorable forward movement of the narrator/protagonist's "flight." Shabine's story effectively becomes a trope for the tensions and complexities of Walcott's relationship to place and the past.

"The Schooner *Flight*" employs a dramatic mode as well. In addition to dramatic monologue, the poem renders Shabine as a character in his own right, marked by his distinctively salty, graphic speech and his sense of theater, as shown by the way he "sets the stage" for his account of the duel with Vince. This is one of the many confrontations in which Shabine becomes involved, climaxing in the conflict with the storm that images a cathartic conflict within himself. Indeed, he seems to see life as conflict: "on one hand Venus, on the other Mars." [24]

To invent and shape one's "life-illusion," or idea of oneself, is of necessity to fashion an idea of one's relationship with one's world and historical contexts. In "The Schooner *Flight*," as is usual with Walcott, the pressure of a personal, even autobiographical, statement is pushing outward to comprehend a region and a people. Shabine's problems and involvements are both personal and communal. While he is very much himself, an individual, his name is generic or representative nonetheless: "the patois for / any red nigger." He is the mulatto, but he is also the West Indies: "I have Dutch, nigger, and English in me, / and either I'm nobody, or I'm a nation." His cry and his quest are at once private and public. If he is fleeing from the difficulty of balancing a mistress against a wife and children, he is also in flight from the difficulty of doing a balancing act among different factions of his audience/society, from the burden of postcolonial disillusionment, from the corruption of the new, native Establishment, and from naive, suicidal gestures of revolution. But even as Shabine flees, he is articulating his soul-wrenching awareness of what he is trying to put behind him. Indeed, that awareness is an ineradicable part of him. He is fleeing from what he loves, for "loving these islands" has been his "load." Alone at the end, by choice, wearing the stoic mask, he can nevertheless say, "I am satisfied / if my hand gave voice to one people's grief." [25] One can almost hear Walcott composing his own epitaph.

The ending of "The Schooner *Flight*" remains problematic, suggesting a paradoxical situation of simultaneous detachment and engagement. Such is the efficacy of the mask. Shabine's flight *is* ostensibly an escape from responsibility, for although he swears that he loves his wife and his children, he leaves them. He enjoys a lonely luxury of contemplation, studying the stars.[26] Still, his personal odyssey is informed by the idea of the odyssey of a people, a *diasporic* people. Whether in flight or quest, Shabine's journey into an uncertain future has to include traveling back into the traumatic West Indian past; he must be submerged in the horrors of West Indian history and *get the bends* in the process.[27] He has to experience imaginatively the "madness" of his (people's) history in order to achieve psychic wholeness. He also has "to know the pain of history words contain,"[28] which is what this poem enacts. Ultimately, the "sea bath" that Shabine ironically anticipated taking turns out to be lustral, while his flight becomes an act of engagement and celebration that leads him to invoke a blessing on his place and people. Although he ends up alone, he nevertheless affirms the ideas of relationship and sharing; although he cultivates a sort of transcendental detachment in an effort "to forget what happiness was," he can't. His song, his story, his fiction of himself, whatever he has learned from the depths of his experience, he offers to his audience, his people: "Shabine sang to you from the depths of the sea."[29]

## Notes

1   Edward Baugh, "Ripening with Walcott," *Caribbean Quarterly* 23 (1977): 84.

2   Derek Walcott, "The Schooner *Flight*," in *The Star-Apple Kingdom* (New York, 1979), 3.

3   Derek Walcott, "Another Life," University of the West Indies Library, Mona, Jamaica, 39.

4   Ibid., 9.

5   Stephen Spender, *World Within World* (London, 1951), viii.

6   Malcolm Lowry, *Hear Us, O Lord from Heaven Thy Dwelling Place* (Philadelphia and New York, 1961), 268. Ortega y Gasset says: "Our life is given to us—we did not give it to ourselves—but it is not given to us ready-made. It is not a thing whose being is fixed once and forever, but a task—something which has to be created—in short, a drama"; see *Man and Crisis*, trans. Mildred Adams (New York, 1962), 159–60. Note how this formulation explicitly accommodates "drama" in the idea of the narrative of self-creation.

7   Quoted in Roy Pascal, *Design and Truth in Autobiography* (London, 1960), 71.

8   Quoted in Richard Murphy, "Fierce Games" (review of Thom Gunn, *Selected Poems 1950–1975*), *New York Review of Books*, 20 March 1980, 28.

9   Derek Walcott, "The Divided Child," in *Another Life* (New York, 1973), 39.

10  Derek Walcott, "Koenig of the River," in *Star-Apple Kingdom*, 43.

11  Derek Walcott, "The Liberator," in *The Fortunate Traveller* (New York, 1981), 52.

12  Derek Walcott, "The Estranging Sea," in *Another Life*, 148.

13  Derek Walcott, "The Man Who Loved Islands," in *Fortunate Traveller*, 37.

14  Derek Walcott, Poem XIII, in *Midsummer* (New York, 1984), 23.

15  Derek Walcott, Poem XXIX, in ibid., 40.

16  Derek Walcott, "The Hotel Normandie Pool," in *Fortunate Traveller*, 65.

17  Walcott, "The Schooner *Flight*," in *Star-Apple Kingdom*, 4.

18  Ibid., 6.

19  Ibid., 4, 14, 18, 8.

20  Lloyd W. Brown, *West Indian Poetry* (Boston, 1978).

21  Derek Walcott, "A Sea-Chantey," in *In A Green Night: Poems 1948–1960* (London, 1962), 64.

22  Walcott, "The Schooner *Flight*," in *Star-Apple Kingdom*, 5, 19.

23  Ibid., 20.

24  Ibid.

25  Ibid., 4, 19.

26  The valedictory tone of the ending is not nearly so marked in another version of the poem that appeared a year after *The Star-Apple Kingdom* was published. In this version, "the black fear of nothing" that threatens Shabine gives way to action-oriented affirmation, "when, out of nothing, the day-hidden stars, / unbidden, but abiding, came"; see *Chant of Saints*, ed. Michael S. Harper and Robert B. Stepto (Urbana/Chicago/London, 1979), 174.

27  "The Sea Is History," as the title of another poem in *The Star-Apple Kingdom* tells us.

28  Walcott, "The Schooner *Flight*," in *Star-Apple Kingdom*, 12.

29  Ibid., 20.

**Gregson Davis**

# "With No Homeric Shadow": The Disavowal of Epic in Derek Walcott's *Omeros*

A la fin tu es las de ce monde ancien

Bergère, ô tour Eiffel le troupeau des ponts bêle ce
  matin.
—Guillaume Apollinaire

The ghost of Homer sings. His words have the sound
of the sea and the cadence of actual speech.
—Marianne Moore

The American poet Marianne Moore opens a famous poem with words that appear, at first reading, both disingenuous and radically subversive:

POETRY
I, too, dislike it: there are things that are
    important beyond all
                              this fiddle.[1]

After this brusque disavowal of poetry—of her own love for her cherished vocation—she proceeds at once to attenuate, if not recant, her opening broadside in a tone of mitigation: "Reading it, however, with a perfect contempt for it, one / discovers in / it after all, a place for the genuine." The rest of the poem provides a veritable catalogue of images, instances of what Moore regards as "genuine." In fine, the reader is first

The *South Atlantic Quarterly* 96:2, Spring 1997.

seduced by an apparently sincere confession of dislike that is implicitly collusive ("I, *too*, dislike it"); but no sooner has this complicity between poet and audience been reinforced by a gnomic declaration ("there are things that are important beyond all / this fiddle") than we are led to an immediate counterassertion or correction—a statement of preference for a truly authentic brand of verse ("a place for the genuine"). We are led, in other words, to revise our reading of the first line and to hear it, in retrospect, as tongue-in-cheek and ironic. In our revised perception we come to realize that the ostensible disavowal of poetry is not, "after all," a blanket dismissal, but rather the first move in a dialectical maneuver the culmination of which is, paradoxically, a profession of faith. "Perfect contempt" turns out to be, surprisingly, a proposed way of "reading" poetry with a discriminating eye for quality. The poem evolves, in effect, into an avowal of what the poet judges to be genuine in the realm of the poetic. She has chosen this rhetorical pathway (disavowal–qualification–avowal) as a subterfuge to guide us to the special place that she has marked out for herself—a place she calls, in the final strophe, "the imaginary garden" of poetry.

Moore's pseudo-disavowal is given a totalistic cast: she archly claims to "dislike" poetry in general. The paradoxical rhetoric of (dis)avowal in Derek Walcott's *Omeros* represents an analogous move, but one by which poetic genre rather than poetry *tout court* is foregrounded. The genre in Walcott's case is the epic. Although this Caribbean poet has explicitly rejected the epic label in published interviews, it is his generic disavowals in *Omeros*—his internal "performative" exclusions—that will be our focus here. As Oliver Taplin has pointed out, Walcott's poem provokes the reader by its length and ambition, as well as the very names of its characters, to make comparisons with Homeric epic.[2] Why then does the narrating voice conspicuously disavow the Greek-epic paradigm at more than one fulcrum point in the poem? Or, to rephrase the question in more narrowly rhetorical terms, what does the narrator gain from invoking Homer while disowning the Homeric genre? This rhetoric of inclusion/exclusion has aesthetic, linguistic, and philosophical implications, among others. Walcott's version of the gambit so brilliantly epitomized in Moore's poem appears to yield an egregious paradox (what Taplin calls "denial" and "contradiction"). Here, I shall attempt to establish a *formal* as well as a *literary-historical* context for the performance of disavowal.

To begin with the literary-historical background to the strategy of disavowal, literary scholars who work in the Greco-Roman tradition conventionally refer to the move as *recusatio* (refusal), and there is by now a voluminous critical literature dissecting the device as practiced most notably by the major Augustan poets: Horace, Vergil, Propertius, and Ovid. The Latin poets, for their part, modeled their conventional (dis)avowals on topoi derived from Greek poets of the Hellenistic period such as Callimachus, who strove to find a "place for the genuine" ostensibly by eschewing Homeric manner and matter. In this Hellenistic and Roman line of tradition, epic grandeur is bypassed, even obliquely denigrated, in favor of small-scale, "light" composition. The internal critical discourse of these Greek and Roman poets in the shadow of Homer is framed in generic terms: the epic is set up as the generic "other" against which the non-epic composer defines his craft. A single, well-known example of the Latin convention may suffice by way of illustration, namely, Ovid's second book of love poems, the *Amores*, which begins with a programmatic reformulation of his generic choice:

> Once, rashly, I sang of war in heaven and giants
> with a hundred arms. My diction soared to the occasion—
>
> the cruel vengeance of Mother Earth, and the piling
> of Pelion upon Ossa upon Olympus.
>
> But while I was busy with Jupiter standing on a storm-cloud,
> thunderbolt at the ready to defend his heaven,
>
> Corinna slammed her door. I dropped the thunderbolt
> and even forgot the Almighty.
>
> Forgive me, Lord. Your weapons couldn't help me.
> That locked door had a far more effective bolt.
>
> I returned to couplets and compliments, my own weapons,
> and broke down its resistance with soft words.[3]

In Ovid's humorous, even parodic, version of the rhetorical convention, the speaker stages an abrupt abandonment of grand themes—metaphorized in Jove's thunderbolt—under the irresistible impact of erotic passion. He opts for light elegy, rather than heavy epic, as the genre best suited to amorous themes. The metaphor of "thundering Jove," incidentally, is appropriated from the prologue to Callimachus's *Aetia*, a Hellenistic text that served as a kind of aesthetic manifesto for an entire generation of Latin poets. The author of the *Amores* is echoing this defining text while reenacting the drama of generic choice in his own programmatic poem.

It would be easy to multiply examples of rhetorical disavowals in ancient and modern European lyric, for the convention is nothing short of ubiquitous in poetry of all periods. What is of interest here is how it functions in the major composition of a contemporary poet who delights in manipulating traditional motifs as a sophisticated means of articulating his own aesthetic. Walcott's move is best clarified by comparison with its deployment in the work of other poets, ancient and modern (insofar as these epithets circumscribe a Eurocentric lyric tradition). As the Apollinaire epigraph indicates, even supposedly iconoclastic precursors of modernism like this poet utilized, consciously or unconsciously, the complex dialectic of rejection and reassimilation: "In the end you are tired of this ancient world. // Shepherdess, O Eiffel Tower, the flock of bridges is bleating this morning."[4] Immediately after bluntly disavowing antiquity (and, by implication, its outmoded generic repertoire) in his first line, the radical poet of "Zone" proceeds, in the second, to invert the ancient pastoral convention that opposes city to country, on his way to defining his own modernist voice. Despite the dismissive opening, this double move is a standard formal ploy in the antique discourse of self-definition. "Self" in such contexts refers, of course, to the artistic persona that is constructed through the performance of writing/reading.

In comparing homologous enactments of disavowal, it is important to consider the contours of the disavowed: the shape and dimensions of the "other" set up as a generic foil to the poet's articulation of his/her project. As our glance at Moore's "Poetry" revealed, the other may, at one extreme, be conceived with such amplitude that all inauthentic "fiddle" is strenuously differentiated from the genuine article; for Apollinaire, the dividing line is drawn so as to exclude (ostensibly) the entire Greco-Roman tradition ("ce monde ancien"). Walcott's frequent deployment of this foil is supremely elastic, so it provides a useful gauge of his virtuosity as it is exercised from the more ample to the more narrow generic horizons.

---

In his exquisite long poem *Another Life*, Walcott deferentially ascribes grandeur of style (a standard feature of epic discourse) to the visual opus of his friend, the painter whom he calls Gregorias:

> Provincialism loves the pseudo-epic,
> so if these heroes have been given a stature
> disproportionate to their cramped lives,
> remember I beheld them at knee-height,
> and that their thunderous exchanges
> rumbled like gods about another life,
> as now, I hope, some child
> ascribes their grandeur to Gregorias.[5]

Striking in this formulation of the conventional poetry/painting comparison is the way in which the postcolonial poet is represented by the infant who hears the dominant European voices as grown-up "thunder" emanating from gigantic figures. (Ovid's metaphor comes to mind.) In the very act of establishing the sound as distant thunder, the speaker expresses the hope that his artist friend will have succeeded in reaching an equivalent resonance, so to speak, in the rival medium of painting. This move of displacement (from Walcott, the aspiring poet, to the artist "Gregorias") is a common feature of the classical convention whereby another contemporary poet and friend is often put forward by the speaker as more suitable for the task of imitating the grand style. Thus the speaker in *Another Life* is already engaged in a process of self-reflection concerning the formation of an authentic voice that has declined to emulate the epic thunderbolt. The effort by Walcott's speaker to hold European canonic grandeur at a distance while acknowledging its power parallels (though perhaps subliminally) the stance of Ovid and the Augustans vis-à-vis Greek models. Both contemporary postcolonial poets and postclassical Latin poets strive to legitimate their own unique voices by claiming distinctness from a remote, Olympian epic manner.

At several sutures in the fabric of *Omeros* a narrative thread appears that is nominally incongruent with Walcott's mode of rewriting the Homeric version of the Helen of Troy myth. This alternating (and alternate) narrative is ascribed to a character named Dennis Plunkett, a former British sergeant-major who has retired to the island of St. Lucia. An amateur historian, Plunkett adopts a project (for him an obsession) that involves discovering suggestive analogies for the grand enterprise of the Trojan War in events of Caribbean colonial history, such as the 1782 naval conflict between the

British and the French known as the Battle of Les Saintes. Plunkett's desire to write a history of St. Lucia along epic lines is rooted in a quasi-literary impulse to read historical parallels in verbal coincidences and wordplays, such as the fact that St. Lucia had acquired the sobriquet the "Helen of the West Indies" because it was a notorious bone of contention between rival colonial powers in the archipelago. Although the narrator appears to distance himself from Plunkett's project (which, ironically, he describes as an attempt to reduce history to metaphor), it is nevertheless given a marked prominence in the poem, thereby posing the tantalizing question of the relationship between the two, generically different narrative strategies. The poet/narrator perhaps comes closest to framing the question in a passage that, openly averring both the convergence and the divergence of the two narrative agendas, takes up the reinvention of the Greek Helen as a Black St. Lucian housemaid:

> Plunkett, in his innocence,
>
> had tried to change History to a metaphor,
> in the name of a housemaid; I, in self-defence,
> altered her opposite. Yet it was all for her.
>
> Except we had used two opposing stratagems
> in praise of her and the island; cannonballs rolled
> in the fort grass were not from Olympian games,
>
> nor the wine-bottle, crusted with its fool's gold,
> from the sunken *Ville de Paris*, legendary
> emblems; nor all their names the forced coincidence
>
> we had made them. There, in her head of ebony,
> there was no real need for the historian's
> remorse, nor for literature's.[6]

What is ostensibly disavowed here is, in fact, a move that is made by both narrative orders (historiographic and literary). Homeric names, and the stories they carry, are shamelessly exploited by both composers, the speaker concedes. This acknowledgment of an underlying convergence, however, also encompasses a disavowal, for the poet/narrator, who has claimed that "forced coincidences" are unnecessary ("there was no real need"), now candidly criticizes a "stratagem" he has also intermittently employed elsewhere in the poem. The rhetorical leverage he gains by this admission and juxtaposition is subtle and effective, allowing him to have his cake and eat it too by an oblique denigration of a pseudo-historian's use of Homeric names as a stratagem of praise without any apparent consciousness that the epicizing of St. Lucia and the ennobling of an actual maid are inherently specious.[7] The well-known Aristotelian dictum that poetry is "more philosophical than history" is latent in the juxtaposition.

Walcott's use of an ersatz historiographer as a generic foil may seem highly contrived and artificial to the reader unfamiliar with its conventional character. An example from a Latin poet whose work mediates Greek models may help to elucidate the rhetorical technique at work in *Omeros*. In addressing a lyric poem to his friend and patron Maecenas, Horace positions him as a potential composer of historical narrative who, he asserts with false modesty, is better equipped than himself to handle epic themes adequately:

> You would not wish me to tune the lyre's gentle strains
> to the drawn-out wars of savage Numantia, nor harsh
> Hannibal, nor the Sicilian sea ruddy
> with Punic blood
>
> nor the wild Lapiths, the wine-distraught Hylaeus,
> and the earth-born brood subdued by Heracles' might
> that caused the gleaming demesne
> of ancient Saturn
>
> to tremble at the danger: surely you, Maecenas,
> would better relate in a historian's prose the wars
> of Caesar, and alien kings dragged by the neck
> through Roman streets;
>
> for my part my Muse has wished me to relate
> Licymnia, my mistress: her sweet songs, her gleaming
> eyes, her constancy throughout our truly
> mutual passion.[8]

In accordance with the ancient convention of the separation of stylistic levels, the Horatian disavowal emphasizes the disparity between historical and lyric discourse by presenting the subject matter—love rather than battles—as the determining factor in the poet's choice of the gentle lyric strain. Walcott's placement of Plunkett operates like Horace's of Maecenas, setting in relief the poet/narrator of *Omeros*, although the generic status of this poem is deliberately left vague and undefined. With the "historical epic" voice of Plunkett contrapuntal to that of the narrator, however, all those "forced coincidences" are an integral part of the polyphonic composition.

An important aspect of the form being delineated here is what we might call the reintegration of a disavowed term. Taplin has shrewdly remarked that although Walcott rejects the epic theme of "battles," *Omeros* contains copious references to figurative "lances."[9] The reintegration, at the figurative level, of matter ostensibly excluded by the speaker is also thoroughly conventional in the *recusatio*.[10] In the work of the Augustan poets, for instance, it is standard for the "recusing" poet to eschew military matter ("kings and battles," in Vergil's summation in the prelude to *Eclogue* 6), but then to reincorporate such matter via metaphor. Thus Ovid, in the poem quoted earlier, reclaims some previously abandoned weapons by transferring them to the erotic sphere: "I returned to couplets and compliments, my own weapons, / and broke down its resistance with soft words." By a similar subterfuge in "Zone," as we have seen, Apollinaire repudiates ancient pastoral in language that figuratively transfers the bleating of sheep to the bridges of modern Paris.

In his many appropriations of epic subject matter, Walcott reveals that he is not actually renouncing "epic" so much as redefining it and, in the process, demonstrating the fundamental fluidity of the whole concept of genre. This metaphorical reclamation of an "epical" allure that is strenuously denied on the literal surface is nowhere more transparent than in the passage in which the griot characterizes the suffering of his people in the Atlantic slave trade:

> But they crossed, they survived. There is the epical splendour.
> Multiply the rain's lances, multiply their ruin,
> the grace born from subtraction as the hold's iron door
>
> rolled over their eyes like pots left out in the rain,
> and the bolt rammed home its echo, the way that thunder-
> claps perpetuate their reverberation.[11]

In the reverberation of the "thunderclap" analogy we may perhaps hear the distant echo of epic disavowals.

In its use of generic foil *Omeros* conjures up many reincarnations of the epic bard.[12] Since the very name is a signifier for the entire epic tradition (including the Homeric poems), we may conceptualize it in terms similar to those Claude Lévi-Strauss used to describe myth: the figure of Omeros consists of all its variants, a rhapsode figure comprising non-European as well as European instances, such as the African griot who recounts the past experiences of the tribe. Late in the poem, the speaker reports a dialogue with a vagrant bard whom he recognizes as a reincarnation of Homer: " 'I saw you in London,' I said, 'sunning on the steps / of St. Martin-in-the-Fields, your dog-eared manuscript / clutched to your heaving chest.' " The bard's reply to the recognition of his timeless identity ends with a disclosure: "a drifter / is the hero of my book."[13] There is an implied convergence between the epic singer/writer and his theme, between the wandering Odysseus and the drifting epic bard who, like Phemius or Demodocus in the Homeric intertexts, does the circuit of the Mycenean courts. Drifting is also a metaphor that relates to the sea and its currents, of course, so the motif of the sea as "fluid" epos is once again emphasized.[14]

It is in the context of such strategic redefinitions of Homeric themes that the speaker utters a startling, even explosive, disavowal in reference to the unnamed book carried by Omeros: " 'I never read it,' / I said. 'Not all the way through.' " It is significant that the initial denial is immediately corrected with "not all the way through," alerting the reader to the hyperbole endemic to virtually all variants of the disavowal gambit—hyperbole that also prepares us, as it does in Moore's poem, for the explicit reading instructions soon to be vouchsafed—here, by Omeros. Responding to the speaker's objections to the divine apparatus in the *Iliad* and the *Odyssey*, Omeros is made to say, "Forget the gods . . . and read the rest." The brusque, charged exchange between the two poets culminates in a revelation that not only negates the hyperbole of "I never read it" but replaces it with a description of Walcott's peculiar relationship to the Homeric text: "I was the freshest of all your readers."[15] Clearly, what occurs through this sleight of hand is that Walcott's own reading of Homer—an underlying aesthetic agenda of the poem—acquires legitimacy, even authentication, from the mouth of "Homer" himself. The poet's stance of disavowal allows him to reposition himself vis-à-vis the tradition, to stake out a claim for the "genuine" and thereby authenticate the aesthetic that governs his reading and, by extension, his rewriting of a canonic text.

The rhetorical structure of "generic disavowals" has a philosophical underpinning that may be framed in terms of the writer's quest for an originary poetic language. Walcott exposes this deeper structure in the same self-reflexive passage in which he compares (and discriminates between) Plunkett's project and the poet's—his own:

> Why not see Helen
>
> as the sun saw her, with no Homeric shadow,
> swinging her plastic sandals on that beach alone,
> as fresh as the sea-wind? Why make the smoke a door? [16]

The question pinpoints the epistemological predicament that constrains all writers, wistfully proposing a "way of seeing" that is an unattainable ideal, given the nature of language: a Helen seen "with no Homeric shadow." In the next subsection, the speaker pursues a self-interrogation that, like all "rhetorical" questions, contains its own answer:

> When would my head shake off its echoes like a horse
>
> shaking off a wreath of flies? When would it stop,
> the echo in the throat, insisting, "Omeros";
> when would I enter that light beyond metaphor? [17]

The desire for a pristine linguistic universe, the "light beyond metaphor," arguably subtends the poem as a whole. From a broader perspective, we may plausibly infer that this desire is ultimately the source of the dynamic of all generic disavowals. In Walcott's poetics, the nexus between the desire to transcend metaphor and the motif of disavowal is by no means confined to the text of *Omeros*. An extremely lucid instance of that nexus is already manifest on the surface of the early poem "Greece." Here, in the compass of two brilliant strophes, the speaker represents himself as climbing a seaside cliff and discarding "a great book" in a purifying gesture that enables him to utter words denuded of intertextual echoes—the very project he reposes, almost poignantly, in *Omeros*. The Homeric corpus, with its burden of echoes, is precisely what is being discarded here:

> The body that I had thrown down at my foot
> was not really a body but a great book

still fluttering like chitons on a frieze,
till wind worked through the binding of its pages
scattering Hector's and Achilles' rages
to white, diminishing scraps, like gulls that ease
past the gray sphinxes of the crouching islands.

I held air without language in my hands.[18]

The cathartic gesture of discarding the Homeric poems leads to the repossession of a pristine, unmediated bond with things ("air without language"), as the poet begins to write, transcribing substantives directly from nature and thereby reinventing the names of things: "Now, crouched before the blank stone, / I wrote the sound for 'sea,' the sign for 'sun.'"[19] This reinventing of lexemes captures the creative vision that may perhaps be most parsimoniously formulated in semiotic terms, namely, the Saussurean axiom of the "arbitrary" nature of the sign, which, along with its corollary the "empty signifier," is strenuously denied by most poets, who endorse the "necessary fiction" that words can and do refer to things in an unmediated relation to which a genuine poet has access. As Walcott phrases it, "I learned what a noun is, writing this book. No one is Adam. A noun is not a name you give something. It is something you watch becoming itself, and you have to have the patience to find out what it is."[20] At the level of discourse as well as at the microlevel of vocabulary, the quest for "the original story," as it is termed in "Greece," is predicated on discarding all prior texts. The reader, no less than the writer, is aware that exorcising a vision of a universe, and a fortiori a linguistic universe, from text (*hors-texte*) is a doomed enterprise, but it is energetically pursued nonetheless by any writer who desires to create Moore's "imaginary gardens with real toads in them."[21]

Walcott's inflection of the quixotic quest for the full signifier ("the sign for 'sun'") may be aptly compared with that of Wallace Stevens. Among the many texts in Stevens's lyric corpus that perform a gesture of disavowal as a precondition for recuperating a lost linguistic plenitude, perhaps the most elucidating for our purposes is "The Man on the Dump." Stevens's speaker represents himself as a post-Romantic poet who finds himself on the dump—a symbolic site on which all prior (Romantic) images of the moon have been discarded. From this vantage point he is empowered to see (and write) the moon "as the moon," thus recouping the putative integrity of the linguistic sign:

Between that disgust and this, between the things
That are on the dump (azaleas and so on)
And those that will be (azaleas and so on),
One feels the purifying change. One rejects
The trash.
          That's the moment when the moon creeps up
To the bubbling of bassoons. That's the time
One looks at the elephant-colorings of tires.
Everything is shed; and the moon comes up as the moon
(All its images are in the dump) and you see
As a man (not like an image of a man),
You see the moon rise in the empty sky.[22]

The fresh vision (and the language in which it takes shape) is here predicated on a prior refusal, on discarding the encrustations of the quintessen-
tial Romantic sign, the moon. Whether or not "The Man on the Dump"
constitutes a conscious intertext for a recurrent strand in the fabric of Walcott's *Omeros*, it is illuminating to compare those passages in which Walcott
reaches for the "light beyond metaphor." In this regard, the words attributed to the persona named Afolabe summarize succinctly, even gnomi-
cally, the insight that underlies and informs the rhetoric of disavowal.
The narrative context is a dialogue between the African Afolabe and his
Caribbean descendant Achille—a dialogue cast in a dreamlike, Vergilian
(read: mediated Homeric) underworld. Achille has spoken of the means
by which he has been transported to his ancestral homeland "by a swift, //
or the shadow of a swift." The attentive reader, immediately recognizing
the muse of Omeros in the recurrent emblem of this seabird, is thereby
alerted to the implications of Afolabe's aphoristic response: "No man loses
his shadow except it is in the night, / and even then his shadow is hidden,
not lost."[23] Walcott's "Homeric shadow" is never lost in *Omeros*; it is only
sporadically occluded. Paradoxically, however, it is most present at those
very moments when its absence is most fervently proclaimed as the object
of the poet's desire.

### Notes

1   Marianne Moore, "Poetry" (longer version), in *The Complete Poems of Marianne Moore*
    (New York, 1981), 266–67.

2  Oliver Taplin, "Derek Walcott's *Omeros* and Derek Walcott's Homer," *Arion* 1 (1991): 213–26.

3  *Ovid's Amores*, trans. Guy Lee (New York, 1968), 59–60 (ll. 11–22).

4  My translation. The French text of these opening lines of "Zone" is from *Guillaume Apollinaire: Oeuvres poétiques*, ed. P. Adéma and M. Décaudin (Paris, 1956), 213.

5  Derek Walcott, "The Divided Child," in *Another Life* (New York, 1973), 41.

6  Derek Walcott, *Omeros* (New York, 1990), 270–71 (6.54.2).

7  Walcott's own words, as quoted in a *New York Times* interview, make the point incisively: "One reason I don't like talking about an epic is that I think it is wrong to try to ennoble people. . . . And just to write history is wrong. History makes similes of people, but these people are their own nouns"; *New York Times*, 9 October 1990, C13.

8  Horace *Carm.* 2.12; my translation. For the unorthodox ascription of Licymnia (the beloved) to the speaker rather than the addressee, see Gregson Davis, "The Persona of Licymnia: A Revaluation of Horace *Carm.* 2.12," *Philologus* 119 (1975): 70–83.

9  Taplin, "Walcott's *Omeros* and Walcott's Homer," 223–24.

10  For a discussion of key Greco-Roman examples of such "incorporation," see Gregson Davis, *Polyhymnia: The Rhetoric of Horatian Lyric Discourse* (Berkeley and Los Angeles, 1991), 30–36.

11  Walcott, *Omeros*, 149 (3.28.1).

12  Cf. Taplin, "Walcott's *Omeros* and Walcott's Homer," 215.

13  Walcott, *Omeros*, 282, 283 (7.56.3).

14  See Marianne Moore's review of Ezra Pound's *Cantos* (from which my epigraph is taken), in *A Marianne Moore Reader: Poems and Essays* (New York, 1961), 149–66.

15  Walcott, *Omeros*, 283 (7.56.3).

16  Ibid., 271 (6.54.2).

17  Ibid., 271 (6.54.3).

18  Derek Walcott, "Greece," in *The Fortunate Traveller* (New York, 1981), 35–36.

19  Ibid., 36.

20  *New York Times*, C13.

21  Moore, "Poetry," in *Complete Poems*, 267.

22  Wallace Stevens, "The Man on the Dump," in *The Palm at the End of the Mind*, ed. Holly Stevens (New York, 1972), 163–64.

23  Walcott, *Omeros*, 138 (3.25.3).

**Carol Dougherty**

# Homer after *Omeros*: Reading a H/Omeric Text

> Whoever has approved this idea of order, of the form of
> European, of English literature will not find it prepos-
> terous that the past should be altered by the present
> as much as the present is directed by the past.
> —T. S. Eliot, "Tradition and the Individual Talent"
>
> I re-entered my reversible world.
> —Derek Walcott, *Omeros*

With his typical fascination with the poly-
valence of language and the significance of
names, Derek Walcott provides an etymology of
the title of his epic early in *Omeros*:

> I said "Omeros,"
>
> and *O* was the conch-shell's invocation,
> *mer* was
> both mother and sea in our Antillean patois,
> *os*, a grey bone, and the white surf as it
> crashes
>
> and spreads its sibilant collar on a lace shore.[1]

Infusing the English transliteration of the Modern Greek pronunciation of the ancient poet's
name with the polylingual sounds of the Carib-

The *South Atlantic Quarterly* 96:2, Spring 1997.
Copyright © 1997 by Duke University Press.

bean Sea, Walcott smoothly intertwines past and present, Greek and Caribbean poetic traditions. The Modern Greek form of Homer's name emphasizes the enduring modernity of this well-told tale, while its antiquity is
captured by the image of "a grey bone." *Mer* carries a triple signification
not only of the mother and the sea but also of the hybrid nature of the
French Creole that makes up just part of the linguistic mélange of the
Caribbean islands.

Etymologies, especially bilingual ones, forge important connections between cultures. They translate a foreign word in terms that make sense
and provide authority to one's own culture. In colonial contexts in particular, bilingual etymologies are traditionally employed as tools of imperial
power—a kind of linguistic colonialism that often accompanies and legiti-
mates the political conquest by which two cultures have been brought into
contact in the first place.[2] The ancient Greeks, for example, colonized Sicily
and southern Italy extensively from the eighth to the sixth centuries B.C.E.,
and many tales that recount these colonial foundations include bilingual
etymologies for native Siceli place-names. One tale translates the local
name for a pair of important Siceli deities (the Palici) as "those who have
returned" (*palin hikousi*). Not only does this particular etymology translate
the local place-name into the Greek language, but it generates a narrative that describes Greek colonial activity in Sicily as an inevitable return.[3]
Thus the Greek translations of Siceli names mirror the act of settlement
itself; both transform the native landscape into a Greek city.

But Walcott's bilingual etymologies in *Omeros* reverse this direction to
discover contemporary colonial meanings in an elite and often imperial
literary tradition.[4] He appropriates the prestigious poetry of antiquity in
his quest to found a Caribbean national epic. Walcott reminds us that the
world of literary and cultural influence is not a one-way mirror, but rather,
as he describes it, "a reversible world." In fact this theme of reciprocity
permeates the poem, as we can see from the opening of book 5:

> I crossed my meridian. Rust terraces, olive trees,
> the grey horns of a port. Then, from a cobbled corner
> of this mud-caked settlement founded by Ulysses—
>
> swifts, launched from the nesting sills of Ulissibona,
> their cries modulated to "Lisbon" as the Mediterranean
> aged into the white Atlantic, their flight, in reverse,

repeating the X of an hourglass, every twitter an aeon
from which a horizon climbed in the upturned vase.
A church clock spun back its helm. Turtleback alleys

crawled from the sea, not towards it, to resettle
in the courtyard under the olives, and a breeze
turned over the leaves to show their silvery metal.

Here, clouds read backwards, muffling the clash
of church bells in cotton.[5]

The swifts chart the linguistic movement from Ulysses to Lisbon (by way of
Ulissibona), from past to present, from the Mediterranean to the Atlantic,
negotiating a path littered with images of the return trip. The hourglass,
the upturned vase, the backward clocks, the turtleback alleys, resettle-
ment—all create the possibility of reversing direction to trace an "X" from
the Old World to the New and back again, offering a model for similarly reciprocal readings of *Omeros* and the Homeric poems. Clearly, Walcott was
influenced by classical (and other) poetic traditions, and the temptation is
always to begin by addressing issues of influence: What is Walcott's relation to Homer and other major literary figures? How has he adapted the
Homeric tradition? Is *Omeros* an "original" poem or an imitation? I want
to resist that impulse and return to Homer, using Walcott's reverse etymologies as a guide, to explore how the language, images, and narrative
of *Omeros* can help open up new ways of reading "backwards." How is our
reading of the *Iliad* and the *Odyssey* now directed by Walcott's epic? What
new texts do we find when we reread the ancient Greek epic poems after
*Omeros*?

New Homeric texts? The prospect is not as unlikely or heretical as it may
sound. Like much of contemporary Caribbean literature, Homeric epic
was originally oral poetry. In spite of popular traditions (both ancient and
modern), Homer was probably not a real historical person, but rather the
name the ancient Greeks associated with the tradition of oral poetry that
survives today in the form of the *Iliad* and the *Odyssey*. These poems, however, comprise just a small portion of the many songs that were composed
and sung for centuries in ancient Greece.[6] We have the titles of at least six
other poems that tell the story of the Trojan War, starting with the *Cypria*,
which recounted the gods' decision to cause the war, and ending with the
return of Odysseus and his eventual death, as told in the *Telegonia*.[7]

This entire epic cycle forms just part of an oral poetic tradition that dates back to the rich and powerful Mycenean palace culture of the sixteenth through twelfth centuries B.C.E. Even after the mysterious destruction of this world, these poems continued to be sung until the archaic period (8th–6th centuries B.C.E.), when, with the introduction of the alphabet, they began to be written down. It was probably not until the fifth century B.C.E., however, under the sponsorship of the Athenian tyrant Hipparchus, that the texts crystallized into what we now know as the *Iliad* and the *Odyssey*.

Like all oral traditions, the flexible nature of Homeric poetry is built into the very details of performance.[8] The oral poet worked with building-blocks of words, phrases, and entire scenes, drawing upon a rich and complex poetic tradition to tell his own story. He never memorized his song in advance, but rather, in an improvisatory process not unlike that of a jazz musician, composed his song on the spot, responding to the circumstances of each occasion and the interests of his audience. In many ways, the *Odyssey* is all about storytelling and full of details on the nature of poetic performance. Odysseus himself weaves together different accounts of his travels, varying them throughout the poem to please or persuade the wealthy and reclusive Phaeacians, a hungry and lawless Cyclops, or his patient and perceptive wife, Penelope. The successful poet is one who can adapt his song to satisfy his audience, and this structural flexibility extended to the larger cultural audience for oral poetry as well.[9]

In archaic Greek society, as well as in other societies, oral poetry served as a source of cultural continuity and identity. It gave the Greeks a context in which to tell stories about, and thus attempt to control, the unstable, even volatile, world in which they lived. The archaic period, when these poems took their current shape, was one of massive change and innovation in Greece. From the eighth to the sixth century B.C.E., the Greeks established trade contacts overseas and settled a remarkable number of colonies; both literacy and coinage had a major impact on economic, political, and literary life. At the same time, the polis, or Greek city-state, developed, fostering a sense of Panhellenic identity.[10] The *Odyssey* in particular reflects the tensions that emerged from a society in flux, drawing upon existing narratives and cultural themes (tales of travel, accounts of ideal worlds, etc.) to provide the Greeks with a way of addressing and accommodating those radical changes.

In other words, in their original, native context, the Homeric poems, just like *Omeros*, comprised an ever-fluid synthesis of stories and traditions that aimed to forge or consolidate a sense of national identity in a time of crisis and change. The authority and fixity with which time and scholarship have invested the Homeric poems obscures their original flexibility and synthetic impulse. Instead of further calcifying these texts, we might do better to draw upon *Omeros* in order to recapture their full narrative potential. Beneath the "master narrative" that frames the *Iliad* as the familiar story of the "wrath of Achilles," and the *Odyssey* as the "return of Odysseus," are a myriad of alternative story paths—other ways the tales might have been told. Working back from *Omeros* to Homer and forward again, hence constituting what we might call the H/Omeric text, we can open up our reading of both poetic traditions to a richer sense of cultures in contact, of imperial conquest, and of the important role played by epic poetry in framing and commemorating those experiences—the fruits of "reading backwards."

≡≡≡≡≡

*Omeros* opens not with Achilles or Odysseus—no Virgilian "arms and the man"—but with Philoctete, who "smiles for the tourists." After showing them how to cut cedars into canoes,

> For some extra silver, under a sea-almond,
> he shows them a scar made by a rusted anchor,
> rolling one trouser-leg up with the rising moan
>
> of a conch.[11]

As an opening detail, the image of the "scar made by a rusted anchor" suggests several avenues for rereading. The scar reminds us that this story has already begun—it already has a rusted, violent past—and sketches out the general direction of a less well-traveled path back to Homer. However important a figure Philoctetes was in Greek mythology and literature, he lurks at the edges of the *Iliad* and the *Odyssey*, denied a central role. In the *Iliad*, he is mentioned only once, in the Catalogue of Ships, and precisely to explain his absence from the war (and, as a result, the poem). The poet, listing the various Greek troops of the coalition that sailed to Troy, identifies Philoctetes' men:

> They who lived about Thaumakia and Methone,
> they who held Meliboia and rugged Olizon,

of their seven ships the leader was Philoktetes
skilled in the bow's work, and aboard each vessel were fifty
oarsmen, each well skilled in the strength of the bow in battle.
Yet he himself lay apart in the island, suffering strong pains,
in Lemnos the sacrosanct, where the sons of the Achaians had
    left him
in agony from the sore bite of the wicked water snake.
There he lay apart in his pain; yet soon the Argives
beside their ships were to remember lord Philoktetes.[12]

The poet emphasizes the stark contrast between the hordes of Greek soldiers enumerated in the catalogue and the solitary Philoctetes, who "lay
apart in his pain." He also gestures toward the end of Philoctetes' story by
alluding to the time when the Argives will remember the abandoned hero.
Moreover, although the poet tells us here that Philoctetes was not part of
the Greek coalition that arrived in Troy, the very nature and structure of
the catalogue implies that the wounded hero could have done so in another
version of the story. The catalogue is a flexible component of oral poetry,
as expandable and contractable as the poet wishes, and this description of
Philoctetes' absence stands as a placeholder for further details and variations on the story. Walcott's early introduction of "Philoctete" into *Omeros*
thus helps us imagine another *"Iliad"* in which "Philoctetes" did sail to
Troy with the others.

Walcott reads between the lines of the Homeric poems to find Philoctetes and return the hero to the epic tradition. The surprise of his initial
appearance is mediated by the fact that he is introduced as a kind of Odysseus—a seafaring man with a scar. Indeed, the scar we find in the opening
pages of *Omeros* is not the traditional mark of Philoctetes, but the definitive sign of the wandering Odysseus. In the *Odyssey*, the hero finally
returns home and, disguised as a beggar, tests the loyalty of his wife and
friends. When, at Penelope's request, Odysseus agrees to let his old nurse,
Eurycleia, bathe him, he suddenly remembers his scar:

                Now Odysseus
was sitting close to the fire, but suddenly turned to the dark side;
for presently he thought in his heart that, as she handled him,
she might be aware of his scar, and all his story might come out.

> She came up close and washed her lord, and at once she recognized
> that scar, which once the boar with his white tusk had inflicted
> on him when he went to Parnassos, to Autolykos and his children.[13]

The scar, indelible trace of a boyhood hunting wound, is the key to the hero's identity in a poem that is all about his beleagured and belated return home to claim his land, his wife, and his name. Note how closely the scar is linked with Odysseus's story: he is afraid that "she might be aware of his scar, and all his story might come out." Furthermore, the sight of the scar marks the moment at which the poem begins to resolve itself: Odysseus reestablishes himself as king of Ithaca; he punishes the suitors and is reunited with Penelope.

By invoking "the scar made by a rusted anchor," Walcott introduces Philoctete as an Odysseus of sorts, while Odysseus's absence from *Omeros* both captures the hero's famed anonymity and love of disguise in the *Odyssey* and compensates for Philoctetes' absence from the Homeric poems. Odysseus may play at being "Nobody" in the famous scene with Polyphemus the Cyclops, but he becomes literally nobody in *Omeros*, where he appears only in the guise of Philoctete—his trademark scar temporarily appropriated by the very man he once abandoned on a desert island.

Philoctetes is traditionally marked not by a scar but by a wound—an open sore in fact, hence an ever-painful, gangrenous, smelly wound that refuses to heal and thus leave a scar. His story is probably best known to us from Sophocles' play, the *Philoctetes*, in which the themes of civilization, alienation, and the nature of heroic behavior are combined. According to tradition, Philoctetes accidentally stumbled into the precinct of a goddess and was bitten by a snake (often a symbol of divine power). The smell and his cries of pain made him intolerable to his companions, who then abandoned him on an island for ten years. Late in the Trojan War, however, Odysseus, the one who had originally marooned Philoctetes, returned to trick him out of his famous bow, for it had been prophesied that Troy would fall only by this weapon.

A Caliban figure within the Greek poetic tradition, Philoctetes embodies the themes of isolation, suffering, and the power of the primitive. His exile has already lasted ten years when Sophocles' play opens with Odysseus's "return" to the deserted island of Lemnos where he abandoned the wounded hero:

> This is it; this Lemnos and its beach
> down to the sea that quite surrounds it; desolate,
> no one sets foot on it; there are no houses.
> This is where I marooned him long ago,
> the son of Poias, the Melian, his foot
> diseased and eaten away with running ulcers.[14]

Philoctetes' isolation (reinforced by Sophocles' making Lemnos uninhabited), together with his dehumanizing wound, characterizes him as the antithesis of civilization. He represents the potential for savage and inhumane behavior that is part of being human, but against which "humanity" is often defined. In Sophocles' play, Neoptolemus speaks with frustration of Philoctetes' inability to forgive: "Your anger has made a savage of you."[15] The story of his exile and subsequent recall to Troy narratively acknowledge the problematic role played by the primitive in any society's attempt to create and maintain a sense of civilization. Troy cannot be conquered without Philoctetes and his bow; civilization can never completely expel the primitive. But perhaps most of all, it is suffering and the ever-painful wound that mark Philoctetes as the quintessentially marginal Greek hero. Philoctetes' own words make the connection:

> Sorrow, sorrow is mine. Suffering has broken me,
> who must live henceforth alone from all the world,
> must live here and die here;
> no longer bringing home food nor winning
> it with strong hands. Unmarked, the crafty words
> of a treacherous heart stole on me. Would I might see him,
> contriver of this trap,
> for as long as I am, condemned to pain.[16]

Precisely because of his pain, Philoctetes is not only condemned to the outer limits of the Greek world, but he is also relegated to the margins of its most famous poems, the *Iliad* and the *Odyssey*. Walcott, however, discovering traces of his presence in the Greek tradition, returns the wounded hero to the center in his Caribbean epic.

In *Omeros*, the mark on Philoctete's shin soon resumes its more familiar shape as an unhealed sore, and this wound then takes on its own larger significance in the overall scheme of Walcott's poem:

                    The itch in the sore
tingles like the tendrils of the anemone,
and the puffed blister of Portuguese man-o'-war.

He believed the swelling came from the chained ankles
of his grandfathers. Or else why was there no cure?[17]

Philoctete's incurable wound and its attendant suffering permeate the poem at many other levels in addition to its role here as testament to the indelible cruelties of slavery—Original Sin, man's degradation of the environment, and so on.[18] Suffering is part of the Caribbean experience, and for Walcott it also comprises the creative process. Major Plunkett, one of Walcott's narrative alter egos, has his own war stories, his own pain:

This wound I have stitched into Plunkett's character.
He has to be wounded, affliction is one theme
of this work, this fiction, since every "I" is a

fiction finally.[19]

Plunkett and, by implication, Walcott create their stories from their pain; fiction is born from affliction.[20] Philoctetes, the wounded and marginalized Homeric hero, thus emerges as a primary player in a modern Caribbean epic, further refining our notions of epic hero and poet.

But there is more to be gained from *Omeros*'s new focus on the Philoctetes figure. Walcott's introduction of Philoctete as an Odysseus figure helps us see, perhaps for the first time, the complicated and interesting relations between Philoctetes and Odysseus that were always already at play in Homer. Philoctetes is mentioned briefly twice in the *Odyssey*: first, in book 3, when Nestor, telling Telemachus about the various fates of the Greeks returning home after the fall of Troy, mentions that Philoctetes returned home safely (3.190); second, when Odysseus, prior to competing in the Phaeacians' athletic games, boasts that he is better at archery than all the other Greeks—all, that is, except Philoctetes:

I know well how to handle the polished bow, and would be
first to strike my man with an arrow aimed at a company
of hostile men, even though many companions were standing
close beside me, and all shooting with bows at the enemies.
There was Philoktetes alone who surpassed me in archery
when we Achaians shot with bows in the Trojan country.[21]

Philoctetes manages to return home, and he is a master archer: the two details that Homer chooses to mention about the absent hero—his return and his skill with the bow—are, in fact, the primary themes of the *Odyssey* and what characterize Odysseus as its hero. As Walcott makes explicit in *Omeros*, Philoctetes' mythological persona is linked in an interesting way, both narratively and structurally, to that of Odysseus, and a careful rereading reveals compelling connections between these two heroes in the Homeric poems as well.

| **Odysseus** | | **Philoctetes** |
|:---:|:---:|:---:|
| home | | exile |
| sea/travel | bow | island/stationary |
| | foot injury | |
| scar | | wound |
| | suffer | |
| travel/knowledge | | isolation/pain |
| civilization | | savagery |

The two heroes are alike in terms of their skill with the bow and their leg injuries. Moreover, each suffers. Philoctetes' pain derives from his open wound; its intolerable stench leads to his exile, which leaves him at the margins of civilization and the story. Odysseus's suffering, however, stems conversely from his prolonged travels and ultimately produces knowledge and the ability to return home. He learns about the minds and cities of many men, and this experience of travel and travail defines him as the civilized hero of intellect, strategy, and the ability to survive. Philoctetes, on the other hand, precisely because of his isolation and cultural deprivation, is associated with nature and the savage side of the human experience. Sophocles' tragedy plays with Philoctetes' image as both heroic antithesis of Odysseus and symbol of the primitive, wild state that must be left behind as part of the rite of passage that all Greek males make as they come of age and assume the status of citizens.[22] In spite of (or perhaps, as Walcott suggests, precisely because of) the polarizing tensions between these two heroes, their stories are inextricably connected; rather than functioning as contrasting mythic types, Philoctetes and Odysseus occupy opposite ends of a continuum that delineates the heroic territory as the space between home and exile, travel and isolation, civilization and savagery. Each figure helps define the boundaries of the other, and fusing them fleshes out the otherwise monolithic characterization of the hero to which Homeric epic tends.

Walcott complicates his heroic composite of Philoctetes and Odysseus even further when, in true ring composition, he returns near the end of *Omeros* to the tourists and photographers, but shifts their focus from Philoctete to Achille, who is furious "at being misunderstood // by a camera for the spelling on his canoe." Like Philoctete, Achille too suffers:

> So an anchor
>
> had hooked its rust in one sufferer, and the scar shows
> on the slit bone still; so work was the prayer of anger
> for a cursing Achille, who refused to strike a pose
>
> for crouching photographers.[23]

Themes of suffering and the sea reappear in this reprise of the rusted scar and anchor, but Walcott now adds Achilles to the already merged heroic figures of Philoctetes and Odysseus, for Achille, too, has a scar that causes him pain. By linking him to Odysseus and Philoctetes as well as to Achilles, Walcott underscores the vulnerability that subtends, yet threatens to undermine, heroic behavior and suggests that the Homeric Achilles has something to add to the civilized heroic status of Odysseus and the primitive power of Philoctetes: "the prayer of anger." "Anger" (*mēnin*), we remember, is the opening word of Achilles' poem, the *Iliad*. Like Odysseus's scar and Philoctetes' wound, anger is Achilles' defining characteristic. It is also the source of his ultimate pain, the loss of Patroclus. And it is this anger that Walcott appropriates at the end of *Omeros*:

> So, if at the day's end
> when they hauled with aching tendons the logged net,
> their palms stinging dry with salt cuts from the stubborn seine,
>
> the tourists came flying to them to capture the scene
> like gulls fighting over a catch, Achille would howl
> at their clacking cameras, and hurl an imagined lance!
>
> It was the scream of a warrior losing his only soul
> to the click of a Cyclops, the eye of its globing lens,
> till they scuttered from his anger as a khaki mongrel

does from a kick. It was the last form of self-defence,
it was the scream of gangrene, and the vine round his heel
with its thorns. Waiters in bow-ties on the terrace

laughed at his anger.[24]

In this one brilliant scene, Philoctetes, Odysseus, and Achilles are col-
lapsed into a single Caribbean epic hero. Achille's scar, like the wound of
Philoctetes, still stings; his anger provokes "the scream of gangrene." Walcott, adding Achilles' figurative sore spot, his anger, to *Omeros*, gives voice
to the pain of the epic hero.

Again, Walcott projects onto a single character (here, Achille) traits that
are represented by separate, though related, heroic identities in Homer.
Philoctetes and Odysseus jointly articulate the complicated relation of
civilization to the primitive, while Achilles and Odysseus individually
represent competing models of the Greek hero: brave, honorable Achilles
fights; tricky, strategic Odysseus travels. Each of these two has his own
poem, unlike Philoctetes, whom Walcott rescues from epic oblivion and
inserts firmly into the middle of *Omeros*, not content to reserve him for a
surprise ending in an epilogue. Walcott centers his own epic on Philoctete,
on issues of suffering and marginality, thus showing us the flip side of the
stories of conquest and imperialism represented by Achilles and Odysseus,
the heroes of the *Iliad* and the *Odyssey*, respectively. What emerges from
our H/Omeric text is a three-dimensional picture of the epic hero, one
that is centered on his weaknesses and that encapsulates the geographical
triangle of this epic tradition: home, Troy, island.

| **Odysseus** | | **Achille/s** |
|---|---|---|
| *Odyssey* | **scar** | *Iliad* |
| home | **heel** | Troy |
| travels | **wound** | fights |
| | **Philoctete/s** | |
| | *Omeros* | |
| | island | |
| | suffers | |

The Homeric poems describe the epic experience from the point of view of those who successfully sail across the seas, conquer foreign lands, and bring home their booty, both human and material. Although both the *Iliad* and the *Odyssey* acknowledge the difficulties and ambiguities of foreign conquest, neither is oriented from the point of view of those who occupy such lands, as *Omeros* is; the Homeric heroes are fighters and adventurers. What Walcott brings to the mix is the postcolonial experience. His poem shifts the emphasis to the heroic experience of living on land that others desire, so his characters embody suffering in radically different ways. Reading backwards opens up new ways of thinking about the Homeric hero; by calling our critical attention to the conspicuous absence of Philoctetes from the *Iliad* and the *Odyssey*, *Omeros* deepens the characters of Odysseus and Achilles. These Homeric heroes help structure Walcott's heroic characters, yet the postcolonial Caribbean experiences of Philoctete and Achille complicate Homer's heroic types. Tales of conquest and adventure combine with the postcolonial point of view to enrich the epic vision of cultural and literary contact.

---

> The ten-years war is finished.
> Helen's hair, a grey cloud.
> Troy, a white ashpit
> by the drizzling sea.
> —Derek Walcott, "Map of the New World"

Helen is always, has always been, many things and thus embodies what men have often characterized as the infinite mystery, ambiguity, or instability of female nature. Wife of Menelaus, lover of Paris; part human, part divine; woman, shade; at Troy, in Egypt, in Greece; passive victim, scheming temptress; waitress, island—Helen is always something else, always the screen upon which others project their fears, needs, and desires. In the following passage, Walcott acknowledges the extent to which poets and historians (like Plunkett) construct their respective images of Helen:

> Except we had used two opposing stratagems
> in praise of her and the island; cannonballs rolled
> in the fort grass were not from Olympian games,

nor the wine-bottle, crusted with its fool's gold,
from the sunken *Ville de Paris*, legendary
emblems; nor all their names the forced coincidence

we had made them. There, in her head of ebony,
there was no real need for the historian's
remorse, nor for literature's. Why not see Helen

as the sun saw her, with no Homeric shadow,
swinging her plastic sandals on that beach alone,
as fresh as the sea-wind? Why make the smoke a door? [25]

The fundamental ambiguity of Helen creates a model for conceptualizing the competing systems of myth and history. Furthermore, as the object of men's desires—Menelaus and Paris, Achille and Plunkett—Helen provides a familiar narrative framework in which to celebrate conflict, whether a full-scale military action like the Trojan War or the Battle of Les Saintes, or, as Walcott tells it, the competition between two fisherman over a local girl:

> Men can kill
> their own brothers in rage, but the madman who tore
> Achille's undershirt from one shoulder also tore
> at his heart. The rage that he felt against Hector
>
> was shame. To go crazy for an old bailing tin
> crusted with rust! The duel of these fishermen
> was over a shadow and its name was Helen. [26]

Helen prompts men to fight each other in order to possess her, and in this context her physical identity represents the land where she lives. Walcott's Helen is both island girl and island: "She lay calm as a port, and a cloud covered her / with my shadow; then a prow with painted eyes / slowly emerged from the fragrant rain of black hair." [27] Plunkett, the local historian, makes the connection between then and now, myth and history, girl and island:

> He smiled at the mythical hallucination
> that went with the name's shadow; the island was once
> named Helen; its Homeric association
>
> rose like smoke from a siege. [28]

Throughout *Omeros*, Walcott plays with the ambiguity of Helen as local island girl and as metaphor for the island itself—both the most beautiful of the Caribbean—and this collocation renders Helen's sexual conquest symbolic of the political domination of her island.

Again, Walcott leads us back to Homer, for in the *Iliad* the war to recapture Helen is also an attempt to conquer Troy. It is a commonplace in Greek myth and literature (as in so many other traditions) to represent political conquest as an act of physical violence, especially sexual violence against women. Pindar's *Pythian* 9, for example, tells the story of the Greek colonial expedition to Cyrene, a city in Libya, as the rape of a young girl, Cyrene, by Apollo, the patron deity of the archaic Greek colonization movement. Women in these narratives represent both the land and those who inhabit it, with their sexual conquest symbolizing the political domination of the land and its people. Similarly, in the *Iliad*, Homer uses the image of the veil a woman wears to protect her face for the ramparts that surround the citadel of Troy. In book 16, just before sending him off to battle, Achilles says wistfully to Patroclus:

> Father Zeus, Athene and Apollo, if only
> not one of all the Trojans could escape destruction, not one
> of the Argives, but you and I could emerge from the slaughter
> so that we two alone could break Troy's hallowed coronal.[29]

This metaphorical unveiling of Troy, with all its intimations of rape, anticipates Andromache's reaction to the news that Hector is dead. She realizes that Troy will soon fall and signals its imminent defeat by throwing away her headdress:

> The darkness of night misted over the eyes of Andromache.
> She fell backward, and gasped the life breath from her, and far off
> threw from her head the shining gear that ordered her headdress,
> the diadem and cap, and the holding-band woven together,
> and the circlet, which Aphrodite the golden once had given her
> on that day when Hektor of the shining helmet led her forth
> from the house of Eëtion, and gave numberless gifts to win her.[30]

Walcott's more explicit use of Helen as an image to blur political and erotic conquest reminds us that not far beneath the surface of the *Iliad*'s celebration of the Greek campaign to recapture a beautiful woman lies a tale of military conquest as well. Structuring the narrative around the desire to recover Helen disguises the Greek mission to capture Troy, and the lamentable fate of Andromache—soon to be enslaved by her conquerers—prefigures that of the city as a whole.

Yet another reading of Helen emerges from the H/Omeric text, for in both poetic traditions, her theft and recovery—an economic exchange gone awry—represents the complications and anxieties that ensue from foreign trade. The fundamental instability of Helen, her failure to remain fixed in the narrative, parallels the volatile and problematic nature of such an exchange; the battle over the beautiful woman becomes a battle for control of foreign commerce. In Walcott's play *The Odyssey*, Helen claims that "the whole thing was not over me but some sea-tax," [31] a quip that encourages us to reread the *Iliad* in the context of trade relations between Greece and Asia Minor at the time of the Homeric poems.

Once the city has fallen, and Helen and the booty captured, the momentum of the Trojan epic shifts to the return home. This is now Penelope's story as much as it is Odysseus's. Women in epic not only represent the conquest, but also the home to which the victors return. *The Iliad* is the story of the quest for Helen, the woman whose face "launched a thousand ships." *The Odyssey*, on the other hand, recounts one man's attempts to return to Penelope, his ever-faithful wife and symbol of home. As Odysseus explains to Calypso, although his wife cannot rival her beauty or grace, "even so, what I want and all my days I pine for / is to go back to my house and see my day of homecoming." [32] Like the home to which the hero desires to return and like her famous weaving, unwoven by night, Penelope must remain unchanged. When Odysseus finally does appear, though in disguise, and tells her stories designed to reassure her that her husband still lives, a simile reveals the degree to which Penelope, and by extension Ithaca, has remained frozen in time during his absence. Here she begins to thaw:

> As she listened her tears ran and her body was melted,
> as the snow melts along the high places of the mountains
> when the West Wind has piled it there, but the South Wind melts it,
> and as it melts the rivers run full flood. It was even
> so that her beautiful cheeks were streaming tears, as Penelope
> wept for her man, who was sitting there by her side. [33]

Penelope, the antithesis of Helen, must remain faithful; at the end of the *Odyssey*, Agamemnon holds her up as the model wife in sharp contrast to Clytemnestra, whose infidelity was just one of the threatening changes he met upon returning home. Penelope represents a sense of community, of social order. In another simile, Odysseus compare her to a good king whose people and crops prosper, reinforcing her identification with home in all its ideal forms—stable, prosperous, productive:

> Lady, no mortal man on the endless earth could have cause
> to find fault with you; your fame goes up into the wide heaven,
> as of some king who, as a blameless man and god-fearing,
> and ruling as lord over many powerful people,
> upholds the way of good government, and the black earth yields him
> barley and wheat, his trees are heavy with fruit, his sheepflocks
> continue to bear young, the sea gives him fish, because of
> his good leadership, and his people prosper under him.[34]

Just as Helen embodies all that men set out to acquire overseas—land, goods, treasure—this simile attributes to Penelope all that Odysseus and the other Greek heroes have been striving for so long to regain.

As antithetical as Helen and Penelope appear to be at first glance, however, Walcott brings them together briefly in the following passage about *his* Helen:

> But the O's encircled her, black as the old tires
> where Hector grew violets, like bubbles in soapy
> water where she scrubbed the ribbed washboard so hard tears
>
> blurred her wrist. Not Helen now, but Penelope,
> in whom a single noon was as long as ten years,
> because he had not come back, because they had gone
>
> from yesterday, because the fishermen's fears
> spread in the surfing trees.[35]

This image of Helen as a Penelope figure, impatiently, tearfully waiting for Hector to return may startle us, but again Walcott suggests an interesting point of departure for thinking about the two heroines of Homeric epic. Although seemingly at odds—one a seductive, home-wrecking temptress, the other a faithful, home-keeping wife—Helen and Penelope occupy positions at either end of a single path between home and abroad. Helen is the woman for whom you leave home, Penelope the woman to whom you return, and male heroic activity (fighting, traveling, conquest, return) occurs in the space between these two women.

| Helen | Men | Penelope |
|---|---|---|
| conquest | travel | home |
| unstable | fight | stable |
| multiple | suffer | same |

In a famous essay on the narrative technique of the *Odyssey*, Erich Auerbach argued that the ability to create "a foreground and background, resulting in the present lying open to the depths of the past, is entirely foreign to the Homeric style; the Homeric style knows only a foreground, only a uniformly illuminated, uniformly objective present." [36] This unidimensionality, due in large part to the contingencies of a true oral style, applies to the Homeric treatment of character as well. The Homeric poems approach the problematics of heroic behavior paratactically, that is, by displaying various themes and qualities embodied in different heroes. Achilles fights, Odysseus travels, Philoctetes suffers. None alone comprises the integrated hero; instead, that concept is articulated between and among them. Walcott's narrative signature, however, is precisely the fusion in one narrative moment of present and past, history and myth, the Aegean and the Caribbean. Accordingly, his polyvalent style produces richly layered, complicated characters whose literary allegiances shift as the narrative demands.

My final rereading of a Homeric text focuses on the attention to poetics that dominates both *Omeros* and the *Odyssey*. Throughout his poetry, but particularly in *Omeros*, Walcott invokes the sea and navigation as metaphors for the poetic process. The sea, we remember, is at the very center of his etymology of the name Omeros. Sea passages become poetic passages as Walcott charts the course of his Caribbean epic. Late in the poem, Seven Seas, one of several poetic figures in *Omeros*, teases the speaker and compares him to the great epic master:

Mark you, *he* does not go; he sends his narrator;
he plays tricks with time because there are two journeys
in every odyssey, one on worried water,

the other crouched and motionless, without noise.
For both, the "I" is a mast; a desk is a raft
for one, foaming with paper, and dipping the beak

of a pen in its foam, while an actual craft
carries the other to cities where people speak
a different language, or look at him differently.[37]

There are two journeys: one made by the hero as he travels from town to town, the other made by the poet as he embarks upon his hero's adventure tale. The hero travels on a real seagoing craft, while the poet conducts his odyssey from his desk—a metaphoric raft. Walcott anchors this navigational imagery firmly in the language of poetry by linking raft and craft here in the alternating scheme of his terza rima.

This nautical metaphor extends beyond language to the very frame of the poem as well. *Omeros* opens with a programmatic passage in which Philocte explains to the tourists how he cuts down the *laurier-cannelles* to make canoes. His prayer for strength here, which recalls the typical Homeric appeal to the Muses, launches Walcott's poetic endeavor.[38] The c/raft metaphor reappears near the end of *Omeros*, with the narrator's announcement that he has finished his poem: "my craft slips the chain of its anchor."[39] In other words, embedded in his poetic craft is a (metaphoric) nautical craft, an image that suggests we revisit Odysseus's maritime adventures and the poem that celebrates them.

The collocation of poetry and sea travel that is made so explicit throughout Walcott's poetry is also at the heart of the *Odyssey*, in which the hero's travels provide both the occasion for his storytelling and the subject matter of the songs: Odysseus's travels produce stories about his travels. Later Greek poets such as Pindar would adopt sea travel as an explicit metaphor for poetry, as we can see from the opening of *Nemean* 5: "I am no sculptor, fashioning statues to stand motionless, fixed to the same base. No, on every merchant ship, on every boat I bid my song go forth from Aegina."[40] Not static like a statue, Pindar's poetic cargo moves; it travels abroad and reaches many audiences, like a commercial boat that carries treasures from one port to another. Both the ship's mobility and the value of its cargo are explicitly at work in Pindar's poem, and, I would suggest (following Walcott's lead), in the *Odyssey* as well. In order to return home to Penelope, Odysseus has to learn to build a raft, one that, like Walcott's poetic craft, represents the art of song.

The technique of oral poetry, as we remember, depends on familiarity with a culture's poetic tradition, often represented as divine inspiration or instruction, and on the ability to improvise within that tradition. Divine instruction and improvisation are at work in book 5 of the *Odyssey*, where Calypso teaches Odysseus how to build a raft so that he can sail away from her island and eventually reach home. While the goddess represents the divine, or traditional, component of c/raft-building, it is Odysseus himself who must build his own c/raft. The Greek word for raft (*schediē*) is etymologically related to the adverb (*schedon*) that means "something close by or near at hand," and the same root underlies a compound (*autoschediazō*) meaning "to improvise." One improvises from things that are at hand, whether one is building a raft or a poem.

As Athena complains to Zeus at the beginning of book 5 (really a second prologue to the *Odyssey*), Odysseus has no ships. He needs to put something together in order to get on with his journey—and his poem. Calypso gives him tools and shows him where to cut down the tall trees, which Odysseus does (just as Philoctete does in *Omeros*), lashing them together. The poet then tells us that Odysseus's raft is as big as a cargo ship: "And as great as is the bottom of a broad cargo-carrying / ship, when a man well skilled in carpentry fashions it, such was / the size of the broad raft made for himself by Odysseus." [41] In the subsequent description of Odysseus's construction of this raft, forms of the verb "to make" (*poieō*, typically used for poetic and other kinds of production) appear four more times in eight lines, followed by a reference to technological skill.

What are the implications of regarding this raft as a metapoetic vehicle? It is interesting that Odysseus's nautical adventure brings him to the court of Alcinous at Phaeacia, where the bulk of his stint as a storyteller occurs, for it is in books 9 to 12 that the voices of Odysseus and the Homeric poet merge. First, Odysseus must build a raft, which then breaks up just as he arrives on shore, symbolic of the constructed and contingent nature of oral poetry: first put together in interesting and useful ways, these bits of songs then get taken apart and reassembled in different arrangements. This is exactly what happens to the stories Odysseus tells the Phaeacians, which are then adapted for those he tells Eumaeus, Telemachus, and Penelope after his return to Ithaca. The improvisational and temporary nature of the raft represents the partial, contingent, and mobile qualities of the poetic truth associated with such tales of wandering. But this raft is as big as a commercial freighter, that is, it can carry considerable cargo from which its traders will profit. Travel, particularly sea travel, yields knowledge or truth as well as commercial profit, and it prompts the telling of stories. In the *Odyssey*, as in *Omeros*, poetic and nautical passages intersect, each fueling the other.

Questions about the relationship between Walcott and Homer are written into the very heart of *Omeros*. The struggle to balance the bountiful *richesse* and the tyrannical authority of literary influence dominates much of Walcott's poetry:

> All that Greek manure under the green bananas,
> under the indigo hills, the rain-rutted road,
> the galvanized village, the myth of rustic manners,
>
> glazed by the transparent page of what I had read.
> What I had read and rewritten till literature
> was guilty as History. When would the sails drop
>
> from my eyes, when would I not hear the Trojan War
> in two fishermen cursing in Ma Kilman's shop? [42]

But the relationship between Homer and Walcott is not merely one in which the din of the past continues to drown out contemporary voices. In fact, responding to the inevitable question about the Homeric influence on *Omeros*, Walcott has said, "The happiness I feel about this book is that I didn't force classical reverberations or stretch to make associations with the classics. It is a book for people, not a conundrum for scholars. *It was as if I was learning to read Homer when I was writing it.*" [43]

Poetic influence flows both ways; all poetic worlds are reversible. *Omeros* certainly belongs to an epic tradition defined in large part by the *Iliad* and the *Odyssey*, but Walcott's poem supplements and reshapes that tradition in turn, helping us learn "to read Homer" again. His fusion of Homeric,

Caribbean, and African traditions (among others) opens up the ancient and authoritative Homeric texts and gently chides us for our previous lack of imagination about them. We certainly can read Homer again, and from now on I will always hear the sounds of two fishermen cursing in Ma Kilman's shop amidst the dust and din of the Trojan War.

### Notes

Versions of this paper were given in an NEH summer seminar, "Classics of Caribbean Literature," organized by Selwyn R. Cudjoe at Wellesley College, and as a lecture at the University of California–Santa Cruz. I would like to thank those who attended for their valuable suggestions and comments, especially Karen Bassi, Selwyn Cudjoe, Gregson Davis, and Joel Krieger.

1    Derek Walcott, *Omeros* (New York, 1993 [1990]), 14 (1.2.3).
2    For further discussion and examples, see S. Greenblatt, "Learning to Curse: Aspects of Linguistic Colonialism in the Sixteenth Century," in *First Images of America: The Impact of the New World on the Old*, 2 vols., ed. F. Chiappelli (Berkeley/Los Angeles/London, 1976), 2: 561–80; and C. Dougherty, "Linguistic Colonialism in Aeschylus' *Aetnaeae*," *Greek, Roman, and Byzantine Studies* 32 (1991): 119–32.
3    For a more detailed discussion, see Dougherty, "Linguistic Colonialism."
4    Another etymology in *Omeros* (and there are many more) supplies an alternative Greek derivation for "democracy": "the Athenian *demos*, / its *demos* demonic and its *ocracy* crass" (Walcott, *Omeros*, 206 [5.41.1]).
5    Ibid., 189 (5.37.1). The swift in particular embodies this potential for reciprocity; see also 238–39 (6.47.3).
6    Both the *Iliad* and the *Odyssey* open with images of multitude—the many-wiled Odysseus learns the ways of many men and cities, the souls of many men are hurled down to Hades—reminding us that these are not the only poems the Greeks knew. Moreover, the *Iliad* and the *Odyssey* are both full of references to poetic traditions that lie outside the poems, such as the songs of Demodocus, Achilles, and Helen, to name just a few.
7    Other surviving titles include the *Aithiopis*, the *Little Iliad*, the *Sack of Ilion*, and the *Returns*.
8    For a general introduction to the techniques of oral poetry, see R. Finnegan, *Oral Poetry: Its Nature, Significance and Social Context* (Cambridge, 1977). On the oral poetics of Homer, see A. B. Lord, *The Singer of Tales* (Cambridge, MA, 1960); R. P. Martin, *The Language of Heroes* (Ithaca, 1989); and G. Nagy, *The Best of the Achaeans* (Baltimore, 1979); and *Pindar's Homer* (Baltimore, 1990).
9    As Telemachus explains to his mother, "People surely always give more applause to that song / which is the latest to circulate among the listeners"; *The Odyssey of Homer*, trans. Richmond Lattimore (New York, 1967), 1.351–52. All quotations will be from this translation.
10   For more on the period, see A. Snodgrass, *Archaic Greece: The Age of Experiment* (Cambridge, 1980); and *Cultural Poetics in Archaic Greece*, ed. C. Dougherty and L. Kurke (New York, 1993).
11   Walcott, *Omeros*, 4 (1.1.1).

12  *The Iliad of Homer*, trans. Richmond Lattimore (Chicago, 1951), 2.716–25. All quotations will be from this translation.

13  Homer *Odyssey* 19.388–94.

14  Sophocles, *Philoctetes*, trans. David Grene, in *Sophocles*, 2 vols., ed. David Grene (Chicago, 1957), 2: ll. 1–7. All quotations will be from this translation; line numbers refer to the Greek text.

15  Ibid., 1321.

16  Ibid., 1101–15.

17  Walcott, *Omeros*, 19 (1.3.3).

18  For connections between wounds and Original Sin, see ibid., 42 (1.7.3); between wounds and damage to the environment, 5 (1.1.1). For discussion of the prevalence of the wound image in the poem as a whole, see R. Terada, *Derek Walcott's Poetry: American Mimicry* (Boston, 1992), 198–99.

19  Walcott, *Omeros*, 28 (1.5.2).

20  See ibid., 171 (4.33.2), 295 (7.59.1).

21  Homer *Odyssey* 8.215–20.

22  See P. Vidal-Naquet, *The Black Hunter: Forms of Thought and Forms of Society in the Greek World*, trans. A. Szegedy-Maszak (Baltimore, 1986), 85–156.

23  Walcott, *Omeros*, 298 (7.59.3).

24  Ibid., 298–99 (7.59.3).

25  Ibid., 271 (6.54.2).

26  Ibid., 16–17 (1.3.1).

27  Ibid., 15 (1.2.3).

28  Ibid., 31 (1.5.3); cf. "Is this chance / or an echo? Paris gives the golden apple, a war is / fought for an island called Helen?" (100 [2.19.1]); see also 288 (7.57.3).

29  Homer *Iliad* 16.97–100.

30  Ibid., 22.466–72.

31  Derek Walcott, *The Odyssey: A Stage Version* (New York, 1993), 31.

32  Homer *Odyssey* 5.219–20.

33  Ibid., 19.204–9.

34  Ibid., 19.107–14.

35  Walcott, *Omeros*, 152–53 (3.29.1).

36  Erich Auerbach, "Odysseus' Scar," in *Mimesis* (Princeton, 1953), 3–23; quotation from 7.

37  Walcott, *Omeros*, 291 (7.58.2).

38  I want to thank Gregson Davis for calling my attention to this passage. The convention of cutting down trees to build a ship at the beginning of an epic recalls the building of the *Argo* and its role at the center of the *Argonautica*, epic and tradition.

39  Walcott, *Omeros*, 323 (7.64.2).

40  Pindar, *Nemean Ode* 5.1–3, in *Pindar's Victory Songs*, trans. Frank J. Nisetich (Baltimore, 1980).

41  Homer *Odyssey* 5.249–51.

42  Walcott, *Omeros*, 271 (6.54.3).

43  Quoted in D. J. R. Bruckner, "A Poem in Homage to an Unwanted Man," in *Critical Perspectives on Derek Walcott*, ed. R. D. Hamner (Washington, 1993), 399; my emphasis.

**Peter Burian**

# "All That Greek Manure under the Green Bananas": Derek Walcott's Odyssey

How could I wish to join a classical tradition when where I was had nothing to do with the vegetation, people or anything remotely referential to Greece or Rome?
—Derek Walcott, 1990

**R**eaders of Derek Walcott's *Omeros*—which, whatever it is, "is not like a rewrite of the *Iliad*"[1]—may have been surprised to find it followed by a play that is explicitly a rewrite of the *Odyssey*. What, beyond a commission from the Royal Shakespeare Company, prompted Walcott to overcome his well-documented diffidence about so direct an attachment to the classical tradition? A partial answer to this question may lie in Walcott's development of Odyssean themes in poems that antedate the play. In this context, Walcott's adaptation of the *Odyssey* emerges as, first and foremost, a continuation of his own artistic quest.[2]

The Caribbean has been at the heart of Walcott's poetic imagination from the beginning, and because that imagination is fiercely honest and intelligent, this has meant giving both Europe and Africa their due. Walcott's love of

The *South Atlantic Quarterly* 96:2, Spring 1997.

the peoples and languages, the landscape and troubled history of the Antilles pulled him in one direction, while his brilliant assimilation of the classical Western education by which the colonial power asserted its cultural hegemony pulled him in another. It is not that Walcott had to choose between them, or that he tried to; rather, he has been able to make the choice, or more precisely the impossibility of making it, one of his most fertile themes. Consider, for example, "Origins," from *Selected Poems* (1964):

> I learnt your annals of ocean,
> Of Hector, bridler of horses,
> Achilles, Aeneas, Ulysses,
> But "Of that fine race of people which came off the mainland
> To greet Christobal as he rounded Icacos,"
> Blank pages turn in the wind.[3]

The tension that animates this passage (and, indeed, the whole of this remarkable poem) is the poet's recognition that he embodies a paradox: a man of European learning living in a world of people largely descended from slaves, including most of his own ancestors, and one from which the indigenous population has been extirpated, leaving hardly a trace. "A Far Cry from Africa," from *In A Green Night* (1962), meditates on the brutal oppression of Africans in the Caribbean and concludes with the poet's personal version of Caliban's complaint:

> I who am poisoned with the blood of both,
> Where shall I turn, divided to the vein?
> I who have cursed
> The drunken officer of British rule, how choose
> Between this Africa and the English tongue I love?
> Betray them both, or give back what they give?
> How can I face such slaughter and be cool?
> How can I turn from Africa and live?[4]

Insofar as such questions can be answered, Walcott's poetry answers them not with *either/or* but with *both/and*. Walcott does not abandon the language and literary culture of the European tradition (there can hardly be a poet writing today with greater erudition), but he supplements, deconstructs, and remakes them with specifically Caribbean sounds, sights, and smells—above all, with a sense of the lived life of his islanders.

Greek myth is one of the mainstays of European tradition that Walcott has found useful at every stage of his career, initially to provide analogues, often ironic, for Caribbean experience, then increasingly to capture a richer and more fully realized sense of the heroic possibilities inherent in that experience. Given the importance of sea, islands, wandering, and return in Walcott's poetic world, it is hardly surprising that the myth of Odysseus recurs more than any other, and in many guises. Sometimes the use made of it is overtly comic, as in these passages from *Another Life* (1973):

> Emanuel
>> Auguste, out in the harbour, lone Odysseus,
>> tattooed ex–merchant sailor, rows alone
>> through the rosebloom of dawn to chuckling oars
>> measured, dip, pentametrical, reciting
>> through narrowed eyes as his blades scissor silk,
>>
>>> "Ah moon / (bend, stroke)
>>> of my delight / (bend, stroke)
>>> that knows no wane.
>>> The moon of heaven / (bend, stroke)
>>> is rising once again,"
>>
>> defiling past Troy town, his rented oars
>> remembering what seas, what smoking shores?
>> . . . .
>> *Heureux qui comme Ulysse,*
>> *ou Capitaine Foquarde,*
>> while his pomegranate-skinned
>> Martiniquan Penelope
>> rocks in her bentwood chair,
>> laughing, stitching ripped knickers,
>> as her coast-threading captain
>> hums, *"La vie c'est un voyage"*
>> and the polished rocker dips
>> as her white burst of laughter
>> drives deep whose prow?[5]

But at least as early as *The Gulf and Other Poems* (1969), we find a more extended and more elaborately metaphorical use of Odyssean themes.

"Homecoming: Anse La Raye" uses the pattern of Odysseus's return to explore the desolate recognition that "there are homecomings without home." While never referring to Odysseus, the poem suggests its Odyssean subtext in various ways. First, it alludes ironically to the uselessness of the myths learned by schoolboys in confronting the reality of this homecoming:

> Whatever else we learned
> at school, like solemn Afro-Greeks eager for grades,
> of Helen and the shades
> of borrowed ancestors,
> there are no rites
> for those who have returned.

Then it evokes a sub-Homeric landscape transposed to the Caribbean shore:

> only this well-known passage
>
> under the coconuts' salt-rusted
> swords, these rotted
> leathery sea-grape leaves,
> the seacrabs' brittle helmets, and
> this barbecue of branches, like the ribs
> of sacrificial oxen on scorched sand.[6]

In such a context, the mention of "this well-known passage" necessarily suggests a literary source as much as a pathway along the shore. But the point is precisely the disjunction between the return imagined through the filter of literature and this one, on "this fish-gut-reeking beach,"

> whose spindly, sugar-headed children race
> pelting up from the shallows
> because your clothes,
> your posture
> seem a tourist's.[7]

The poet, like Odysseus, at first does not recognize his kingdom and is not recognized in turn. He "hoped it would mean something to declare / today, I am your poet, yours," but instead is cursed by the children and ignored by the "dead / fishermen . . . / eating their islands," except for one, who

> with a politician's
> ignorant, sweet smile, nods,
> as if all fate
> swayed in his lifted hand.[8]

The would-be politician with his inflated sense of self-importance suggests yet one more aspect of the alienation that robs this return of any sense of homecoming. The poet who would sing to his people discovers that either they have changed or his perception of them has, and that he, too, has changed in their eyes. The desolation, the bitterness of this poem lies precisely in the speaker's recognition that to those he meets, and finally to himself, he seems not so much an exile coming home as just a wanderer.

Odysseus returns in his own right with a similar sense of unease in "Sea Grapes," the title poem of Walcott's 1976 collection. This poem imagines that "a schooner beating up the Caribbean // for home, could be Odysseus," but an Odysseus whose love for son and wife are, paradoxically, "like the adulterer hearing Nausicaa's name / in every gull's outcry." Odysseus is thus made the emblem of a consciousness at war with itself. This "ancient war / between obsession and responsibility" is identified with the Trojan War, or more precisely with the poetic tradition it engendered, for it "has been the same // since Troy sighed its last flame,"

> and the blind giant's boulder heaved the trough
> from whose groundswell the great hexameters come
> to the conclusions of exhausted surf.
>
> The classics can console. But not enough.[9]

So the poem ends. Waves of Homeric verse have spent themselves on the shore, reminders that the anguish of living and loving is a constant, whether in the Caribbean or the Aegean. The final line, like a receding tide, withdraws any facile solace. The schooner, "tired of islands," sails "for home"; the islander who stands on shore "wriggl[es] on his sandals to walk home." The poem translates them both to the realm of myth, of art, and then reminds us that myth and art are insufficient for the peace we seek.

======

The poem that most fully develops Walcott's Odyssean themes, up to *Omeros* at any rate, is "The Schooner *Flight*," from *The Star-Apple King-*

*dom* (1979), the dramatic monologue of Shabine, poor mulatto seaman, exile, and poet of sea and islands, of freedom and loss. Again, the *Odyssey* is merely adumbrated, but, as we shall see, it is no loose analogy to call Shabine a West Indian Odysseus. This poem takes a decisive step toward *Omeros* and, less directly, toward Walcott's stage version of the *Odyssey*. Shabine speaks (or rather writes, for "The Schooner *Flight*" presents itself as his writing) in a poetic dialect which, like the *Kunstsprache* of the Homeric poems, is not the spoken language of a particular place or time but an amalgam of vernacular and literary idioms with an enormous range and power. Walcott had been using the full linguistic resources of St. Lucia and Trinidad—French Creole as well as Black dialects of English—in drama since his folk plays of the 1950s. His preface to the volume collecting these plays, together with the somewhat later *Dream on Monkey Mountain*, articulates Walcott's ambition to find a language of liberation for the dispossessed Blacks of the New World, "a language that went beyond mimicry, a dialect which had the force of revelation as it invented names for things, one which finally settled on its own mode of inflection, and which began to create an oral culture of chants, jokes, folk-songs and fables."

> It did not matter how rhetorical, how dramatically heightened the language was if its tone were true, whether its subject was the rise and fall of a Haitian king or a small-island fisherman, and the only way to re-create this language was to share in the torture of its articulation. This did not mean the jettisoning of "culture" but, by the writer's making creative use of his schizophrenia, an electric fusion of the old and the new.[10]

This seems to me to express the salient quality of Shabine's language and of much of the language that would give *Omeros* and Walcott's *Odyssey* their particular electricity.

The language of "The Schooner *Flight*" encompasses the explicitly literary and full-throttled Romantic eloquence.[11] Its matrix, however, is the speech of an islander known by a nickname that is "the patois for / any red nigger," but who has also "had a sound colonial education"; the poem, for all its evocation of voice, is Shabine's writing. Indeed, this text keeps asserting its own textuality. Shabine is a serious poet, one who goes so far as to stab the ship's cook "right in the plump of his calf" when he mocks Shabine's poems: "none of them go fuck with my poetry again."[12] Like

Odysseus, he is the bard of his own voyage, and he makes his poetic ambition explicit in regard to this very poem:

> You ever look up from some lonely beach
> and see a far schooner? Well, when I write
> this poem, each phrase go be soaked in salt;
> I go draw and knot every line as tight
> as ropes in this rigging; in simple speech
> my common language go be the wind,
> my pages the sails of the schooner *Flight*.[13]

The poem begins with Shabine leaving home to ship on the *Flight*, a schooner whose name initially seems to suggest escape. Shabine is deserting his woman, Maria Concepcion, as he had earlier left his wife and children, but what we learn in the course of the poem suggests that his flight is something far more complex than escape. Shabine is going into exile and already grieving for his loss. Departing in a "route taxi," he reports, "I look in the rearview and see a man / exactly like me, and the man was weeping / for the houses, the streets, that whole fucking island." This elegiac theme is one central current of the poem; the other is a theme of search, of flight not away but toward. By the end of "The Schooner *Flight*," Shabine's vision has grown to encompass all the islands of the archipelago in a benediction, indeed to imagine the earth itself as "one / island in archipelagoes of stars." In this context, Shabine's quest is expressed both as poetic longing ("I am satisfied / if my hand gave voice to one people's grief") and as longing for an unattainable but endlessly alluring ideal:

> the flight to a target whose aim we'll never know,
> vain search for one island that heals with its harbour
> and a guiltless horizon, where the almond's shadow
> doesn't injure the sand. There are so many islands![14]

This is a version of the outward flight of Dante's or Tennyson's Ulysses, but a version grounded nonetheless in the specific realities of Caribbean history and politics. Shabine is disillusioned by the corruption of the new political class that has taken power since Independence and that has no use for the likes of him: "I had no nation now but the imagination. / After the white man, the niggers didn't want me / when the power swing to their side." The larger sweep of history, on the other hand, means misprision by a racist caste system ("I met History once, but he ain't recognize me"), which ironically has given Shabine the tools of his art: "But that's all them bastards have left us: words."[15] He is the poet as Caribbean Everyman, Everyman as Caribbean poet:

> I'm just a red nigger who love the sea,
> I had a sound colonial education,
> I have Dutch, nigger, and English in me,
> and either I'm nobody, or I'm a nation.[16]

"I'm nobody" strikes an Odyssean note, of course, and there are a number of such echoes in this poem. For example, Shabine's vision of the Middle Passage in "The Schooner *Flight*" parallels Odysseus's calling up of the shades in *Odyssey* 11, with a crucial difference:

> Next we pass slave ships. Flags of all nations,
> our fathers below deck too deep, I suppose,
> to hear us shouting. So we stop shouting. Who knows
> who his grandfather is, much less his name?[17]

Odysseus encounters the shades of his fallen comrades and of his mother, who answer his questions and offer their advice. Shabine and his fellow sailors receive no reply from their anonymous forefathers, who do not hear their cries. This inability to make contact with one's ancestors is capped by a question that recalls Telemachus's words to Athena (*Odyssey* 1.216): "No man yet has known for sure who his father is"—an expression of uncertainty about his ability to be a son worthy of Odysseus. Similarly, Shabine's surviving a storm at sea both suggests and varies the Greek hero's surviving shipwreck and reaching the island of the Phaeacians (*Odyssey* 5 and 6). The storm itself is recounted in terms that evoke the New Testament rather than Homeric epic: the captain, "crucify to his post, . . . hold[ing] fast / to that wheel, man, like the cross held Jesus," until "the noon sea get calm as Thy Kingdom come." But with the return of calm, Shabine imagines the face of his beloved Maria Concepcion as a nubile Nausicaa celebrating her marriage with the sea, "then drifting away / in the widening lace of her bridal train / with white gulls her bridesmaids, till she was gone."[18] Shabine himself is a version of the naked Odysseus receiving clothes laundered in the rain that now falls gently, "like a girl showering":

> I finish dream;
> whatever the rain wash and the sun iron:
> the white clouds, the sea and sky with one seam,
> is clothes enough for my nakedness.[19]

But if Maria Concepcion is a Nausicaa, she is also Shabine's true Penelope, the focus of his longing and his constant muse, her likeness inscribed in sea and sky:

> I knew when dark-haired evening put on
> her bright silk at sunset, and, folding the sea,
> sidled under the sheet with her starry laugh,
> that there'd be no rest, there'd be no forgetting.[20]

---

The very title of Walcott's long poem *Omeros* (the modern Greek name for Homer) suggests that a synthesis of Caribbean and Aegean will be central to its thematics and poetics. *Omeros* is not, however, directly dependent on the Homeric poems for its narrative matter or manner, and the invocations of the *Iliad* and the *Odyssey* (in names, by allusion, and through general similarities of situation) are not without their ambiguities and tensions. At a certain point, late in the poem, the narrator is disturbed to find "all that Greek manure under the green bananas" and asks himself:

> When would the sails drop
>
> from my eyes, when would I not hear the Trojan War
> in two fishermen cursing in Ma Kilman's shop?
> When would my head shake off its echoes like a horse
>
> shaking off a wreath of flies? When would it stop,
> the echo in the throat, insisting, "Omeros";
> when would I enter that light beyond metaphor?[21]

Such a Platonic quest seems doomed. In any case, the lines themselves provide a kind of answer in the audacity of their combination of hexameter-like movement with a version of Dantean terza rima: Walcott's sensibility is so fully formed by the grand traditions of European literature that "the transparent page of what I had read" (as he calls it in the same passage) has become the indispensable vehicle of his art. But Walcott has also claimed the freedom "to make what I wanted of it, or / what I thought was wanted."[22] In short, tradition is not, in Walcott's poetic practice, a strait-jacket for thought but a basic, if perhaps perilous, resource of expression. In any case, even if *Omeros* is Homeric only in limited and sometimes equivocal ways, it is manifestly haunted by the figure of Homer.

To describe every "echo . . . insisting, 'Omeros,'" or for that matter just the echoes that implicate the *Odyssey* directly, would go far beyond the scope of this essay.[23] One quintessentially Odyssean theme appears in a number of guises in *Omeros*, however, and constitutes an animating principle, namely, the Telemachus motif—the search by sons for fathers and by fathers for sons. Achille's psychic journey to Africa while "in the sta-sis of sunstroke" exemplifies Walcott's complex treatment of this theme: Achille is a Odysseus and the voyage is his *nostos*, his return home; at the same time, he is a Telemachus in search of his father; both aspects are explicit in *Omeros*. The breakers, "Ithaca's or Africa's," that swept Achille along made him feel that "he was headed home," but at the same time he "saw the ghost / of his father's face shoot up at the end of the line. // Then, for the first time, he asked himself who he was."[24] When Achille reached Africa, it seemed alien and scary, "like the African movies / he had yelped at in childhood," until God (speaking in St. Lucian Creole!) gave him per-mission to come home. Only then did Achille experience

> the homesick shame
> and pain of his Africa. His heart and his bare head
>
> were bursting as he tried to remember the name
> of the river- and tree-god in which he steered,
> whose hollow body carried him to the settlement ahead.[25]

Names as tokens not only of recognition but of belonging are impor-tant, too, in the encounter with Afolabe, the man whom Achille instantly recognizes as "himself in his father." Afolabe asks him the meaning of the name "they call you," but Achille does not know. For him, it is an entirely arbitrary designation. Afolabe in turn has forgotten the name that he him-self gave to his son, and so has forgotten him: "And you, nameless son, are only the ghost // of a name. Why did I never miss you until you returned? / Why haven't I missed you, my son, until you were lost?"[26] Achille sets about learning his lost past. A griot, a "white-eyed storyteller" like Homer, includes a version of Achille's history among his tales, the tale of a man

who the serpent-god conducted miles off his course
for some blasphemous offence and how he would pay for it

by forgetting his parents, his tribe, and his own spirit
for an albino god.[27]

Achille foresees the full horror implicit in this tale, the enslavement to come, and not only grieves for his father but shares his grief in advance: "The son's grief was the father's, the father's his son's." And their mourning is not just for themselves but for the destruction of a whole world: "So there went the Ashanti one way, the Mandingo another, / the Ibo another, the Guinea. Now each man was a nation / in himself, without mother, father, brother."[28] One is reminded of Shabine's "either I'm nobody, or I'm a nation." *Omeros*, like the *Odyssey*, raises the question of what home means, but it does so in the context of the destruction of cultures and the erasure of identity. Achille's *nostos*, his successful search for his father, is a mixed blessing: the source of "that dawn-sadness which ghosts have for their graves,"[29] since he knows now how much he has lost, but also the source of strength and pride. As Achille returns to port, he watches a black frigate bird stealing fish from white gulls and says:

> "The black bugger beautiful,
> though!" The mate nodded, and Achille felt the phrase lift
>
> his heart as high as the bird whose wings wrote the word
> "Afolabe," in the letters of the sea-swift.
> "The king going home," he said.[30]

The search for the father extends in *Omeros* in a number of directions. Major Plunkett, who has settled on St. Lucia in retirement from the British army, is devoted to his beloved Maud and his historical obsessions, lacking only a son and heir. He finds one when his research into the Battle of Les Saintes (1782), which restored the island to the British, uncovers a long-lost Plunkett:

> This was his search's end. He had come far enough
>
> to find a namesake and a son. *Aetat xix.*
> Nineteen. Midshipman. From the horned sea, at sunrise
> in the first breeze of landfall, drowned![31]

Plunkett, like Achille, goes in search of roots, but what he finds is the descendant he desires and, at the same time, the sorrow of losing him.[32] On the other hand, the narrator, identified in many ways with the author, is still coming to terms with a role reversal that has made him "both father and son" to his own parents. Visiting his mother in her nursing home, he tries to rekindle her failing memory by asserting the identity that she gave him, but has forgotten:

> Her days were dim as dusk. There were no more hours.
>
> From her cupped sleep, she wavered with recognition.
> I would bring my face closer to hers and catch the
> scent of her age.
>        "Who am I? Mama, I'm your son."
> "My son." She nodded.
>        "You have two, and a daughter.
> And a lot of grandchildren," I shouted. "A lot to
> remember."
>        "A lot." She nodded, as she fought her
> memory. "Sometimes I ask myself who I am."[33]

It is a touching scene, the poignancy increased by the trace in the narrator's gestures of Odysseus's failed attempts to embrace his dead mother in *Odyssey* 11 and by the echo in his mother's response of the young Telemachus's uncertainties.

The narrator's search for his father is played out on the literal level, so to speak, by an encounter with the apparition of his dead father and, on the figurative level, by encounters with the apparition of Omeros. The two levels are united by issues of poetic paternity. The encounter with the poet's literal father, explicitly identified as "Warwick," centers on their common writing of verse. Warwick says:

> "In this pale blue notebook where you found my verses"—
> my father smiled—"I appeared to make your life's choice,
> and the calling that you practise both reverses
>
> and honours mine from the moment it blent with yours.
> Now that you are twice my age, which is the boy's,
> which the father's?"
>        "Sir"—I swallowed—"they are one voice."[34]

The passage mingles reversals and honors in striking ways. The son is now twice the age of the dead father, and his verse has far outstripped the father's, who "wrote with the heart / of an amateur." Is the son, then, the father of this father whom his own vision and verse conjure up for us? On the other hand, the assertion that his father's and his own voice are one suggests a nervous desire for the father's approval as well as recognition of his inspiration and a desire to follow in his footsteps.

Omeros appears as the narrator–poet's spiritual father in a paradigm adapted from Dante's *Comedy*: the elder poet guides the younger poet–narrator through the underworld. For Dante, "Omero poeta sovrano" (*Inferno* 4.88) was but a luminous name, but in *Omeros* Homer plays Vergil to Walcott's Dante. The choice is overdetermined, to say the least. Since Homer is one of the wellsprings of what we recognize as the Western tradition, Walcott's self-conscious assertion of his role in that tradition invites the highest expectations by implicitly inviting comparison with one of its most esteemed representatives. Beyond that, however, Walcott exploits the tradition of Homer as blind bard and wanderer, often mistreated, at times reduced to begging for his bread. We meet him in this guise "on the steps / of St. Martin-in-the-Fields" in London, we hear his voice from the mouth of a tent in a ruined Indian camp, and we recognize him in other figures as well, such as the "white-eyed storyteller" in Africa and the blind Seven Seas on St. Lucia. Thus a paradigmatic figure of Western high culture becomes a paradigm of the Wise Man of traditional societies and forges a bond with those so often oppressed by and despised in the deeds and words of the West. In an episode that evokes the shape-shifting Proteus of *Odyssey* 4, the Greek bard appears on the shore of St. Lucia as a marble bust, acquires a body, and then merges in some mysterious way with Seven Seas:

> So one changed from marble with a dripping chiton
> in the early morning on that harp-wired sand
> to a foam-headed fisherman in his white, torn
>
> undershirt, but both of them had the look of men
> whose skins are preserved in salt, whose accents were born
> from guttural shoal, whose vision was wide as rain.[35]

This alternation of identities is not simply another way of suggesting parallels between the Caribbean and Aegean worlds; it asserts the equal claim of the Caribbean to Homer's legacy, to be subject and locus of the creative vision symbolized by the blindness of both singers.

It is as poets, then, that the narrator and Omeros meet, and the meeting is charmingly staged as the sort of embarrassing encounter a younger writer might have with one of his more famous elders. The narrator confesses that he has not read all of Omeros's work, and the poet's withering glance prompts him to stumble on:

> "Those gods with hyphens, like Hollywood producers,"
> I heard my mouth babbling as ice glazed over my chest.
> "The gods and the demi-gods aren't much use to us."
> "Forget the gods," Omeros growled, "and read the rest."[36]

But by the time they have boarded the black canoe that will take them to the underworld, their rapport is such that Omeros, sensing how deeply his companion loves the island, announces, "We will both praise it now." At first, the narrator cannot speak, but soon he finds his voice and joins it to the bard's. It is worth noting, however, that, unlike the "one voice" with which he has said his own and Warwick's verses speak, his voice remains distinct from that of Omeros, which seems to dominate:

> . . . I heard my own thin voice riding on his praise.
>
> . . . .
>
> My voice was going
> under the strength of his voice, which carried so far
> that a black frigate heard it, steadying its wing.[37]

The paternal role of Omeros in the relationship of the two poets is emphasized again in the brilliantly wrought, brief "*Inferno.*" When they reach the "selfish phantoms" of the poets, Omeros saves the narrator from slipping into their pit:

> And that was where I had come from. Pride in my craft.
> Elevating myself. I slid, and kept falling
>
> towards the shit they stewed in; all the poets laughed,
> jeering with dripping fingers; then Omeros gripped
> my hand in enclosing marble and his strength moved
>
> me away from that crowd, or else I might have slipped
> to that backbiting circle, mockers and self-loved.[38]

Paradoxically, then, the patriarch of the remote and formal epic saves his spiritual son from "elevating" himself too high; the master craftsman teaches him not to take too much pride in his craft.

In a larger sense, another seeming paradox may help us to understand the role Walcott has carved out for Homer in the cultural synthesis that sustains his creative work. Apropos *Omeros*, Walcott has remarked, "Part of what I'm saying in the book is that the Greeks were the niggers of the Mediterranean,"[39] referring to the unexpected gaudiness of Greek taste revealed by archaeology: the brightly painted stones of the temples and statues, the use of sumptuous purple and gold, and so on. But the analogy could be extended to the situation of those who produced the *Iliad* and the *Odyssey*—descendants of displaced Ionians driven across the sea by the Dorians who conquered Greece at the end of the Mycenean era. Might this be what draws a poet writing in and of the postcolonial West Indies to the remote and heroic world of the Trojan War? One social function of Homeric epic was to create a past in which the Ionians were not exiles but conquerors, thus asserting the rightful primacy of the audience's ancestors among the Greeks and fostering a sense of solidarity within the diaspora. Without trying to delimit the social function of postcolonial literature, one can recognize in Walcott's work, as in that of many of his contemporaries, an analogous struggle to fashion a useable past and to come to terms with a racial and cultural identity that history has seemingly rendered marginal. The unspoken triumph of Greek epic is that it enabled the defeated Ionians to reconquer Greece not by war but with Homer's art.

But in saying this we must also recognize the counterbalance of two other, equally striking aspects of the Homeric tradition: generosity of spirit and breadth of vision. However flawed and doomed Hector and his cause are shown to be, the *Iliad* never allows us to gloat at Troy's undoing or to lose our intimate sense of the Trojans' humanity and courage. And no matter how intent the *Odyssey* is on home and the hero's return, it also honors his—and our—desire to know "the cities and the minds of men." Both of these qualities are manifest on almost every page of *Omeros*. Walcott's poem does not flinch from the depiction of human suffering on a massive scale, whether as the consequence of colonial pillage in the Caribbean, ruthless expansionism on the Great Plains, the enslavement and sale of the peoples of Africa, or the greed of Caribbean developers. Yet, for all that, there is a consistent balance of judgment that can, for example, appreciate the humanity of colonials such as the Plunketts. (Indeed, Maud Plunkett is perhaps the most thoroughly sympathetic character of the whole poem.) After all, the poetic tradition of *Omeros* and the language(s) in which it is written are part of the colonial inheritance.

Recognition of the composite character of Caribbean culture is itself a link to the world of the ancient Aegean, an island world open to the winds of trade and subject to the whims of conquerors. If the metaphors of journey and home constitute the most obvious contribution of the *Odyssey* to *Omeros*, Walcott's voyages are not only those of his "heroes" but those of nations, and they raise the question of home—where it might be and what it might mean in a world of displacement and deracination. Equally Odyssean, however, is the joy one can take in the verdant beauty of the islands and in the discovery of what lies beyond them.

≡≡≡

Finally, a few words about Walcott's *Odyssey*: in light of the Odyssean thematics of Walcott's poetry, early and late, a dramatization in verse of the Homeric epic seems not so much a detour as a continuation of the voyage. Walcott's play begins with a blind Black singer called Billy Blue doing a riff on the *Odyssey*'s famous opening:

> Gone sing 'bout that man because his stories please us,
> Who saw trials and tempests for ten years after Troy.

> I'm Blind Billy Blue, my main man's sea-smart Odysseus,
> Who the God of the Sea drove crazy and tried to destroy.[40]

One contrast with *Omeros* is apparent, but so is a parallel: instead of an ancient Greek bard as the presiding spirit of a contemporary Caribbean tale, Walcott's *Odyssey* features a Caribbean singer as master of ceremonies for a Greek epic drama. And Billy Blue does more than introduce and comment on the action in his own persona; the almost mystical alternation in *Omeros* between the identities of Omeros and Seven Seas reappears here as Billy's impersonation of the Homeric bards Phemius and Demodocus. Walcott extends his palimpsestic vision of human experience, simply reversing its terms. In his poems, the ancient Aegean and its myths provide an artistic and historical mirror; in his play, the Caribbean and the contemporary world are shadows behind an ancient Greek surface.

Spatial and temporal disjunctions work in Walcott's *Odyssey* much as they do in many of his longer poems. The play extends the horizons of Homeric representation in a number of directions, especially by allowing the adventures among monsters and magicians that Odysseus himself narrates in Homer's *Odyssey* 9–11 to be fully realized as dramatic episodes.

Walcott's Cyclops, for example, is a cross between King Ubu and Big Brother, presiding over a police state where thinking is punished by death; Circe, whose island is a brothel where men become beasts, eventually leads Odysseus to the margin of the underworld through a Shango possession rite; and Hades itself is a spectral underground station, an effective evocation of missed connections.

Many elements of Odysseus's character—resourcefulness, yearning for home and for Penelope, even his appetites and passion for gain—are taken over or elaborated in Walcott's play. But it also reflects a distinctly modern sensibility and preoccupations found elsewhere in his oeuvre. One thing that sits oddly with the Homeric hero is the edge of sexual guilt that Walcott has imported into Odysseus's relations with Circe, Calypso, and even Nausicaa. Penelope plays her traditional role but also with a striking difference: at the end of the play, she questions the violence naturalized and even celebrated in epic. She almost stops the show by objecting to Odysseus's slaughter of the suitors and by refusing to accept this bloody avenger as her long-lost husband. Even though the impasse is soon resolved in the Homeric way, with Penelope's test of the bed, we have been forcefully reminded of a difference between Homer's values and those we profess.

These few hints will, I hope, point to a way of reading Walcott's *Odyssey* not simply as an adaptation of Homer but as a poetic drama that fully belongs to the Walcott canon. "All that Greek manure," a typically witty and ambiguous metaphor, does point, after all, to one of the most important sources of enrichment for the soil in which Walcott's imagination took root.

**Notes**

1   J. P. White, "An Interview with Derek Walcott" (1990), in *Conversations with Derek Walcott*, ed. William Baer (Jackson, MS, 1996), 151–74; quotation from 173.

2   Derek Walcott, *The Odyssey: A Stage Version* (New York, 1993). The play premiered in a Royal Shakespeare Company production at Stratford-upon-Avon, 2 July 1992; for reviews, see *Theatre Record* 12 (1992): 850–55.

3   Derek Walcott, "Origins," in *Collected Poems 1948–1984* (New York, 1986), 11.

4   Derek Walcott, "A Far Cry from Africa," in *Collected Poems*, 18.

5   Derek Walcott, "The Divided Child," in *Collected Poems*, 160, 181.

6   Derek Walcott, "Homecoming: Anse La Raye," in *Collected Poems*, 127.

7   Ibid., 127–28.

8   Ibid., 128–29.

9   Derek Walcott, "Sea Grapes," in *Collected Poems*, 297.

10  Derek Walcott, "What the Twilight Says: An Overture," in *Dream on Monkey Mountain and Other Plays* (New York, 1970), 3–40; quotation from 17.

11  See Nancy Schoenberger, "An Interview with Derek Walcott" (1983), in Baer, ed., *Conversations*, 86–94, in which Walcott describes the poem's opening as a deliberate "votive acknowledgment," like the opening of *Piers the Plowman* (92). Here are the two openings, for comparison:

> In idle August, while the sea soft,
> and leaves of brown islands stick to the rim
> of this Caribbean, I blow out the light
> by the dreamless face of Maria Concepcion
> to ship as a seaman on the schooner *Flight*.
> . . . .
>
> In a somer sesoun, whanne softe was the sonne,
> I shop me in-to a shroud, as I a shep were;
> In abite as an ermyte, unholy of werkis,
> I wente wyde in this world, wondris to here.

References and allusions in "The Schooner *Flight*" (*Collected Poems*, 345–61) range from the New Testament to Alexander Blok's narrative poem of the Russian Revolution *The Twelve*!

See also Charles H. Rowell, "An Interview with Derek Walcott" (1987), in Baer, ed., *Conversations*, 122–54, in which Walcott remarks, "There are passages, I think, in 'The Schooner *Flight*' that seem to me a little too elevated" (130).

12  Walcott, "Schooner *Flight*," 346, 355.

13  Ibid., 347.

14  Ibid., 361, 360, 361.

15  Ibid., 350.

16  Ibid., 346.

17  Ibid., 353.

18  Ibid., 359, 360.

19  Ibid., 360.

20  Ibid., 346.

21  Derek Walcott, *Omeros* (New York, 1990), 271 (6.54.3).

22  Ibid., 271–72 (6.54.3).

23  It is perhaps worth noting that the poem's primary Homeric "references," at least in terms of names and situations, are Iliadic, or to the Trojan War itself rather than its aftermath. There are, however, repeated brief allusions to figures such as Circe (ibid., 64 [1.11.1], 96 [2.18.1], 154–55 [3.29.3], 202–3 [5.40.2]) and the Cyclops (13 [1.2.2], 46 [1.8.2], 201 [5.39.3]—James Joyce with his "eye-patch"!—299 [7.59.3]).

24  Ibid., 131 (2.24.3), 130 (2.24.2).

25  Ibid., 133, 134 (3.25.1).

26  Ibid., 136 (3.25.2), 137 (3.25.3), 138–39 (3.25.3).

27  Ibid., 139 (3.26.1).

28  Ibid., 146 (3.27.2), 150 (3.28.1).

29  Ibid., 141 (3.26.2).

30  Ibid., 158–59 (3.30.2).

31  Ibid., 94 (2.17.3).

32  Plunkett also figures briefly as the narrator–poet's surrogate father. After Maud's death, the narrator observes that "there was Plunkett in my father, much as there was / my mother in Maud," and he pictures himself as the "changing shadow of Telemachus" to Plunkett's "khaki Ulysses." The Odyssean family is completed by a reference to "the one pattern of Maud's fabulous quilt," evoking Penelope's weaving (ibid., 263 [6.52.3]).

33  Ibid., 166 (3.32.1).

34  Ibid., 68 (1.12.1).

35  Ibid., 281 (7.56.1).

36  Ibid., 283 (7.56.3).

37  Ibid., 286, 287 (7.57.1).

38  Ibid., 293 (7.58.3).

39  Robert Brown and Cheryl Johnson, "Thinking Poetry: An Interview with Derek Walcott" (1990), in Baer, ed., *Conversations*, 175–88; quotation from 183.

40  Walcott, *Odyssey*, 1.

# Notes on Contributors

EDWARD BAUGH is Professor of English at the Mona, Jamaica, campus of the University of the West Indies. The author of several articles on Walcott as well as *Derek Walcott: Memory as Vision* (1978), he is currently working on a comprehensive study of the poet for the Cambridge University Press series on African and Caribbean writers.

PETER BURIAN, Professor of Classical and Comparative Literatures at Duke University, edits the Oxford Greek Tragedy in New Translations series, to which he most recently contributed the introduction and notes for Euripides' *Ion* (1996). "On Being a Political Animal in the Academic Zoo" appeared in *The Academic's Handbook* (1995), while "Myth and Muthos" and "Tragedy for Stages and Screens" are forthcoming in *The Cambridge Companion to Greek Tragedy*.

GREGSON DAVIS, a native of Antigua, is Andrew W. Mellon Distinguished Professor of Humanities at Duke University, where he teaches in the Classical Studies department and the Program in Literature. His publications include *Polyhymnia: The Rhetoric of Horatian Lyric Discourse* (1991) and a collection of translations and commentary, *Non-Vicious Circle: Twenty Poems of Aimé Césaire* (1984). *Aimé Césaire* is forthcoming in the Cambridge Studies in African and Caribbean Literature series.

CAROL DOUGHERTY, Associate Professor of Greek and Latin at Wellesley College, is the author of *The Poetics of Colonization: From City to Text in Archaic Greece* (1993) and the coeditor of *Cultural Poetics in Archaic Greece: Cult, Performance, Politics* (1993). Her "Democratic Contradictions and the Synoptic Illusion of Euripides' *Ion*" appeared in *Dēmokratia: A Conversation on Democracies, Ancient and Modern*, edited by J. Ober and C. Hedrick (1996).

JOSEPH FARRELL teaches in the Classical Studies department at the University of Pennsylvania. He is the author of *Vergil's Georgics and the Traditions of Ancient Epic* (1991) and *Latin Language and Latin Culture*, forthcoming in the Cambridge University Press series Roman Literature and Its Contexts.

JUDITH HARRIS, Assistant Professor of English at George Washington University, has published essays and poetry in *The American Scholar*, *Tikkun*, and the *Journal of Psychoanalysis and Social Change*.

TIMOTHY HOFMEISTER, Associate Professor and Chair of the Department of Classical Studies, Denison University, was a 1995/96 Blegen Research Fellow at Vassar College. "The Wolf and the Hare: Epic Expansion and Contextualization in Derek Walcott's *Omeros*" appeared in the *International Journal of the Classical Tradition* (1996), and "Polis and Oikoumene in Menander" is forthcoming in *The City as Comedy: Fictions of the Polis on the Greek Comic Stage*, edited by Gregory Dobrov (University of North Carolina Press).

DEREK WALCOTT, who now resides on the island of St. Lucia (where he was born in 1930), was awarded the 1992 Nobel Prize in Literature. His many volumes of poetry and plays include *Collected Poems: 1948–1984* (1986), *Omeros* (1990), and *The Odyssey: A Stage Version* (1993), which was commissioned and produced by the Royal Shakespeare Company in 1992. A new collection of poems, *The Bounty*, will be published in June by Farrar, Straus and Giroux.

PETER WEISS
# THE
# AESTHETICS
# OF
# RESISTANCE

A novel in three volumes:

vol. I  summer 1997
vol. II summer 1998
vol. III spring 1999

translated from the German by Joachim Neugroschel

"Ever since *Marat/Sade*, Weiss had written work dealing with some
of the main questions of his time. His preoccupations eventually led
to an epic novel about fascism and the fight against it. As Haug and
Maase have stated, it became a *Jahrhundertbuch* (book of the
century) . . . an undertaking in which an entire (European) epoch
and its historical background were re-created" — Robert Cohen,
*Understanding Peter Weiss.*
vol. I ISBN 0-944624-33-2,  $33.95 hardcover

## Maisonneuve Press
P.O. Box 2980
Washington, DC 20013-2980
tel 301-277-7505
fax 301-277-2467
e-mail r-merrill@mica.edu
a limited number of review copies are now available to qualified reviewers.